Your

Freeness, Loveliness, and Divineness

ROAUF

Absolute Author
Publishing House

Your Freeness, Loveliness, and Divineness
Roauf Khalil Aqayi
Copyright 2019

Publisher: Absolute Author Publishing House
Editor: Dr. Melissa Caudle
Cover Designer: Roauf Khalil Aqayi

ISBN: 978-1-951028-29-9

Library of Congress Cataloging-in-Publication-Data

Library of Congress Control Number: 2019920755

Your Freeness, Loveliness, and Divineness/Roauf
    p. cm.

ISBN: **978-1-951028-29-9**

  1. Self-help   2. Spirituality

PRINTED IN THE UNITED STATES OF AMERICA

TABLE OF CONTENTS

Preface

This book contains a collection of aphorisms based on my inner inspirations. Every aphorism indirectly expresses concepts that are like a piece of a universal puzzle of my life and yours.

As you read the book, forget my words and look for authentic concepts deep within your heart and soul. In your mind, put each puzzle piece in its place to see a full picture of the book's general concepts and to understand the inexpressible truth that I didn't find any word to say.

I have nothing to teach you beyond the words; I want to show you the way to experience your true freeness. I want my heart to be a mirror to reflect your true being and your loveliness. My soul amorously worships the divineness that is your true being -- the same person who is also part of my heart and soul.

I wait for the day that this inexpressible truth will be revealed, and our oneness will be manifested, and our divine lovemaking will begin.

You and I have come and will go, but our love and oneness are always permanent in a timeless path.

I am waiting for you along this path to be your fellow traveler, to create a better life and a more beautiful world for each other and for future generations of humankind.

And now our journey begins.

Roauf Khalil Aqayi
www.Roauf.com

Your Freeness

1

The best service of every person in the community of mankind is to be active as much as possible in the direction of his/her interests, talents and goals with an attitude based on respecting human rights in the best way possible.

2

The people of developing and least developed countries are not all satisfied with their existing conditions. However, there are many people with vast thoughts and deep feelings about life and the world and humanity who are stuck in their present condition. They need those who can understand and save them. Then, they can help and welcome them to a better world and life.

3

The opinion of most people is not always right or better than yours. The essence of parliament and collective democracy, and so on, have problems.

It is wrong the majoritarianism dominates society, not a meritocracy system and specialism.

If the majority were wiser, the innovative and creative people like Gandhi and Einstein, etc. could not have changed the world, and the past inefficient process of the public should continue.

Of course, these developments have been widely accepted in desperation by the public.

This sort of meritocracy, regardless of public opinion in specialized fields, has not yet become a global culture.

Governing, based on the majority's voting, is the dictatorship of the majority against the minority. The fairness is based on a meritocracy system and the total votes of the experts in each field, not the blind majority voting on specific and specialized issues.

Some people imagine that if an unlimited expression of love prevails in society, anarchy occurs; and everybody exploits this opportunity for sex and fraud.

Of course, earlier, perhaps in some cases, this can be seen, but the culture of expression of love will shape up gradually.

In the future, a new era will come. That's when our future generations will laugh at our current civilization, fanaticism, and our lack of feelings. They will believe that the leaders and rulers of today's humanity have often been crazy by injecting delusive values into people's minds and hearts.

Then we will have leaders and managers who will understand unconditional love and will strive to rebuild the social values on this principle.

We have always learned to choose a few incomplete and unaware people and make them our boss allowing them to decide about our lives and millions of others' lives. All of this is while there is no one to watch over all their actions.

These heads of our nations, like everyone else, have made wrong decisions and actions, which may not be compensated, and maybe they will never be accountable.

One day will come that our future generations will laugh at our current beliefs.

A society based on unconditional love is the minimum thing that we need to create.

When this extraordinary thing is done, a new horizon opens to us, and we will understand values beyond love.

If we have not yet been able to imagine beyond love, it is because our societies have remained at the stage of accepting love.

For centuries, we deviated from trying to experience a love-based world and for this reason; we have not been able to perceive and experience a vision more magnificent than love.

9

Each person must find and manifest his/her inner values and truth -- the values of society must be shaped in harmony with the valid manifested values of the people.

The generalization and imposition of the values of several people (whether positive or negative) are not correct for the whole society. In fact, it is worthless.

10

If we help and love each other unconditionally, our society and our life (in appearance and inside) is paradise.

If we help and love each other conditionally, our society and our life (in appearance) are beautiful and (inside) ugly.

If we do not help and do not love each other, our society and our life (in appearance and inside) are Hell.

Just our thoughts and behaviors have caused some societies to be like Hell and other societies to have a beautiful appearance but lacking on the inside.

We are the only ones who can transform society into paradise by changing our thoughts and behaviors.

11

We do not need any leader in the world, but we need people who can be a practical model to others moving toward better decision-making and a better life. The practical models can make us aware of our inner leader, and therefore they will have the most impact on our lives.

12

Our community and our parents have taught us a lot of wrong things with conditional love.

It is time for us to learn something better with our unconditional love for ourselves and others.

13

The circumstances we face or the kind of encounter between others and us is the reflection of the quality of unity of humans, creatures, and our social personality, and not our individual personality.

For example, a child who grew up in a wealthy family could gain more success despite having more defects and negative behaviors.

A child who grew up in a low-income family could not achieve significant success despite having more positive behaviors and talents.

Also, the behavior of others in different parts of the world varies with us, while we may not change. So different situations are not mirrored for our personality and behavior.

A child who is killed or raped may not have committed any fault and has not committed an act of injustice to justify the punishment of an individual's cause and effect.

14

We often accept that others are less valuable. That our gender, race, beliefs, family, relatives, close friends, and people like us in general are more valuable, important, and superior.

This didactic is unrealistic, and we believe it according to the suggestions of the family and community. (This belief is a license for hatred and war or unpleasant life with a fake peace and coexistence.)

The life, death, health, success, and transcendence of all of us (directly or indirectly) are dependent on each other. And at the same time, despite having individual independence, we are a unified whole.

We need a free society to have more personal independence and freedom and unlimited growth, transcendence, and success in life.

And we need to love others unconditionally because we need a loving community, so others can accept and love us, and be able to see our common points and strengthen our positive features.

Like freedom, to love and to be loved are the most important needs of every human being. When we love others unconditionally, we create such a community for "ourselves."

Our true self-interests are located in the path of our collective interests. This means unconditional love for others is based on self-love unconditionally.

In such a world and society, regardless of any belief, race, or gender, each of us and those whom we love are accepted, loved, valued, and like anyone else from the united human society, respected.

15

Each human has many positive and negative points in his/her life.

We only can hate others if we focus on their shortcomings, weaknesses, and ugliness without trying to find and help them to solve their problems and needs. We inadvertently force them to conceal their true selves from us. As a result, non-growing individuals will live around us, which will prevent our growth and transcendence.

But a loving person unconsciously focuses on the strengths and attractiveness of others and encourages them to feel good about themselves. They enable others to demonstrate, nurture, reinforce their true talents and abilities, and, ultimately, unconsciously provide a better environment for the one who loves them. The repetitions of this process lead to the formation of a loving community and culture.

On the contrary to folk imagination, ordinary people cannot understand better the value of great people, but there are great people like Martin Luther King and Mahatma Gandhi who can understand better the values of other people. The behavior of great men is always more conscious, more transparent, more humble, and friendlier than unsuccessful humans, and of course, according to the real-life art, not as a performing art.

A lover and a great man or woman are not someone who should be loved by others, but someone who loves others unconditionally.

The biggest secret of lovely people is based on the same principle.

16

Most of our activities seem to be logical, but they are based on specific feelings that can be positive or negative.

The solution to the problems of the world is not hostility or to fight against beliefs that are false to us. Most of our beliefs are not logical and cannot be erased with any logic.

Our beliefs, right or wrong, are based on our most profound feelings that have been suggested in a quasi-hypnotic situation by our parents and society since our childhood.

Science and logic can affect the appearance of human behavior, but they do not solve the most deep-seated social issues of human society.

When one person is in love with everyone else, usually, in this situation, logic is almost ineffective, and less attention is paid to disagreements. This is negative according to logic.

Of course, real love also has tremendous benefits. Being in love is a kind of inner revolution in the face of the past suggested feelings and beliefs we were taught. It is a revolution that transforms our rotten and fanatical beliefs into something new and quite different.

If you've already fallen in love with those you hated before, then you can better understand this subject.

The most crucial benefit of love is its aliveness. Love is not a dead belief. To sustain the manifestation of love, we need to pay attention to these two things:

1. At every moment, there must be a revolution in our minds and emotions to sustain the manifestation of love.

2. Love must be unconditional to overcome the limiting beliefs of others and undesirable conditions.

In other words, unconditional love means a revolution in our minds and feelings at every moment of life, and as we progress to the path of unity.

We need to allow ourselves to love unconditionally and to be a practical model in the path of reprogramming the feelings and the collective subconscious mind of our humankind to create a loving world.

Billions of people live in non-free countries. There are many outstanding people in these countries. Because of their differences with their community, they are limited in their own country and imprisoned. Because they were born into a non-liberal country, they have no right to travel, live, and work in many countries around the world.

There are, of course, many people in those countries who have little understanding of freedom and human rights.

Now is the time for the awareness of human societies and the collapse of a dictatorship culture; not only dictators.

After the *Internet* and the *Web*, this is philanthropy, love, and developing the awareness of people around the world that can reduce the boundary between human beings.

18

The birth of a child, without a formal marriage, and special rules, cannot be negative because in the past, maybe one of our fathers and mothers could have been born in the same way.

Marriage based on religion, law, and tradition is only a social value and contract and does not represent the truth.

19

Have our good and humanitarian thoughts, emotions, speeches, and deeds always had a good result for us?

Are others like a mirror for us? If we see unpleasant behaviors by others, is this the result of our false beliefs and practices?

Do not judge quickly because the issue is not simple.

But why is this wrong? I'll ask a few questions:

- Does a child who is raped face the result of his/her immoral behavior?

- Does anyone such as Mahatma Gandhi, who was murdered, commit violent behaviors?

- Had the winner of the Nobel Peace Prize in a Chinese prison committed inhuman acts?

- If anyone born into a low-income family who has been deprived of many facilities, do they deserve fewer things than others?

- A person who was born into a dictatorship society and cannot travel freely to many countries in the world, is he/she a criminal and should be limited like a criminal?

- Was anyone who lost his/her life to save others, a threat to humans?

- If a child dies or is crippled because of an earthquake or another natural disaster, has he or she committed a big mistake that deserves such a punishment?

- And millions of other examples ...

Of course, up to 50%, I believe that the quality of our life depends on the type of our thoughts and feelings and our behavior.

But we must note that social, environmental, and global conditions have a significant impact on the results of personal activities.

In free and humane societies, our thoughts and behavior often have a more significant impact on society, and in inhuman and dictatorship societies, our thoughts and behaviors may be largely defeated and limited.

To have global thoughts and emotions, we need to pay attention to different situations in the world. For example, a palm tree in the mountains cannot grow, and this is not due to tree disease.

If for all the world's people, there is an entirely free environment and the right to choose equality, I believe that people face only the result of their thoughts and behaviors. However, this is not the case at this moment. Such a thing can be realized in an unconditional love-based world that is without borders.

In general, the notion that we are individuals who are lonely, and each one of us is responsible for his/her behavior and life is a mistake that is inherited from our family and society.

As a particular disease can hurt us or cause us to die, each one of us either can harass or kill each other. At the same time, we can love each other and save and take each other away from inner and outer dangers.

Each of us is a part of the whole unit.

If there are deficiencies and problems in our lives or in others, this reflects weakness, ignorance, and lack of attention of us and the whole human community.

All of us are responsible to each other.

Believing in this subject is not just having a superficial idea and confessing it.

In the same way that we can lose our health and even our lives by not preventing and neglecting a dangerous disease, the same way with the lack of prevention and neglect of the problems of others, we may endanger our lives.

Sitting back and waiting for the positive waves of our thoughts and emotions to be spread throughout the world is not enough. Instead, they must also be manifested in our actions and behaviors.

Unconditional love means perceiving our oneness, despite having full individual independence, accepting practical responsibility for it, and practical help for expanding freedom and equal right to choose in our and others' lives.

20

The human community can be like a world masterpiece of painting.

Each one of us in the human community may have a different color, race, language, gender, feelings, thoughts, and properties, but when each one of us based on his/her talents and interests is in his/her place, each one will be part of the world's masterpiece.

Each one will be like a point in a masterpiece of artwork by the oneness and nature. A real painter enjoys harmony among assorted colors, roles, and forms.

In the same way, when we can enjoy the harmony and connection between various human beings as we reach the stage to love unconditionally.

Also, unconditional love can be strengthened in our being when we can help others to flourish and foster their talents and interests.

We create a global masterpiece by enjoying each other's existence and helping each other to flourish and grow our talents and interests and our original identity.

Only with having a few inconsistent points, the value of a global masterpiece will be decreased to millions of times less.

Unconditional love means trying to coordinate and blossom each individual in any part of the world.

Everyone creates her/his own inner world. It is not supposed for anyone to put other people in the same way. It is our life that should be a model for others to show them how they can create the masterpiece of their inner world, and eventually, the conditions to be ready for the manifestation of the masterpiece of the creation of humankind in the physical world.

21

The biggest obstacles to our success are in our minds and hearts.

The people who their inner world is not free and lovely; in non-free societies, they may deviate from their goals and talents. In free societies, due to the small amount of their mental and emotional capacity, they may not be able to tolerate all aspects of freedom.

To maintain their psychological and emotional security, and to prevent any change and collapse of their beliefs and personality, they, with pessimism, try to limit themselves and their communications and unknowingly make obstacles blocking their success.

By understanding the thoughts, feelings, beliefs, culture, knowledge, and experiences of others in distinct parts of the world, we can make our inner world rich, broad, and free.

The people who their inner world is free and lovely; they are remarkably diverse and attractive people because they have a place for many people within themselves. Others feel that they are valuable, respectable, and lovely alongside them.

They allow the various personalities within themselves to express themselves with an equal right to choose. For this reason, by relying on their harmonious inner world, they can move on the path toward their goals with their whole being and with a beyond imagination power.

Such individuals are trying to respect equal rights to choose freedom and love in their inner world. These are the ones who can criticize themselves, and they will be delighted if others inform them about their mistakes. Why? Because they know when they are aware of their mistakes, they can correct themselves and move toward the path of success.

Of course, for the stability of this inner world and the non-diversion of the path to success, they will ignore the low-minded, illogical, and prejudiced notions.

Such individuals in a limited and non-liberal society may face an intellectual and emotional conflict with the society, which can be very severe and feel suicidal. On the other hand, they can resist a variety of community problems and pressures by relying on their inner freedom and power and even have a positive impact on many people.

The same people in free societies can be manifested in the form of unique, emotional, phenomenally successful, and genius individuals.

When we understand the true meaning of life, we are going to suffer a severe shock because we realize that many of the things we were thinking were valuable, all of them are illusions.

The golden palace of our thoughts, feelings, and delusional beliefs will suddenly collapse in ourselves.

An inner guide is deep inside the existence of all of us. Some people, instead of paying attention to it to change and choose a better life, try to strangle the voice of the inner guide for a lifetime.

Will the world go away if we close our eyes? Absolutely not!

The truth does not change by denying and trying to suppress our inner guide.

It does not matter if our social conditions are good or bad. If we want to have a worthwhile life, you and I have no choice but to be a great man or woman. But how? By understanding others, self-development, unconditional love, and philanthropy.

The sun does not need the light and heat of other stars to exist. In the same way, one who can love unconditionally does not need a reward, affection, and love from others because they are part of the original features of such a person.

Yet, without the coordination and support of others, or in other words, without the coordination and effects of other stars and planets, the suns will also be deviated and destroyed.

We are related to each other, whether we like it or not.

23

Democracy is a culture. If a country is free, but it does not have such a culture, that country may suffer from another chaos or dictatorship.

24

You do not need to be a chef to know if a meal is delicious or not.

Similarly, you do not need to be a psychologist or philosopher to understand the sincerity of others' thoughts and feelings.

Some people may be silent, but in any case, they know how honest and sincere your words and deeds are.

When you try to be sincere and honest in your speech and behavior, you consider others to be very conscious and worthwhile people, and you respect their intelligence.

Do not be deceived by the silence or the negative appearance of others! Surely, the most stupid and ignorant people understand your sincerity and respect; and even these people may transform into your supporters one day.

But more importantly, with honesty and intimacy, you allow your inner wisdom to erupt and make smooth the path of your growth and transcendence.

25

We create our destiny and culture in our thoughts and hearts.

Those who only want to change the politics, laws, and appearances of society, all their efforts are condemned to failure.

Do not be deceived by appearances of revolutions and political changes. Democracy in free countries began with the thoughts and hearts of its people, not merely the social and political appearance changes.

Maybe your friends, family, and the people around you have chosen negative thoughts, feelings, and beliefs resulting in a humiliating life.

Instead of extreme compassion and sympathy, separate your path from theirs' and choose positive thoughts, emotions, and beliefs.

Respect your friends, family, and the people around you and love them. However, you cannot help them, and you will also ruin your own life if instead of choosing your own life, you follow them blindly and participate in their sadness and discomfort.

If you want to help your loved ones, do not immerse yourself in their pain and suffering, but try to solve such problems with humanitarian thoughts, emotions, and beliefs.

Fake great men want to see the truth for you.

True great men try to open your inner eyes straight to the truth.

28

An ordinary human being is an effect of the world's environmental conditions.

A great man is an observer and a cause for change in the world.

29

In general, free-minded people, in a free society, or low-minded people in a closed society, may not have massive social problems.

However, if your mind and emotions stray far from social values, you will face terrible problems.

Once you understand the unity between yourself, humans and the world, your inner power will be more than the force of the environmental conditions. You can have an extremely positive, humanitarian, and infinite thoughts and feelings in the worst, hateful, and limited circumstances.

Most importantly, you can maintain your harmony in a very intense contradiction between the inner world and the outer world.

30

I reject the personal Karma at a high spiritual level. Why? Because this law is utterly meaningless in the world of oneness.

I will give you three examples.

Is a person who is a political or religious leader of millions of people, good or evil, really millions of times more worthy than other people?

If a person who has billions of dollars of income, is his/her activity worth millions of times more than the work and efforts of other people?

A person who was born in a dictatorship country may not have the right to travel, work and live freely in most parts of the world, and she/he is deprived of thousands of different human rights. Does this mean that a person born in a free country is hundreds of times more valuable than a person who was born in a non-free country?

If your answer to each one of these three questions is negative, then you may doubt personal karma.

31

Karma is a relative and variable law and has different meanings in diverse cultures; it is different from the universal law of cause and effect.

If you can understand the oneness aspect, you will accept the universal law of cause and effect, not Karma.

All human beings and creatures are directly and indirectly related to each other in the world, and absolute good and evil are meaningless.

Both people like Martin Luther King and Adolf Hitler are part of our oneness.

For example, the value of a child living in North Korea, as a slave, in this age is the same as a child living in America. None of them deserves distress.

One is the weakness of our unity, and the other is the strength of our unity.

Transcendence and perception of unity based on the past and future are an illusion. Only the true present moment is in accordance with the truth and the oneness.

Karma, in some cultures, is an excuse to deny our responsibility to other parts of our oneness.

32

In the past, based on Karma, we believed African Americans and the indigenous peoples of the Americas were lesser valuable people.

In this age, based on Karma, we still believe some people, nations, and groups on planet earth are less valuable and we think they deserve suffering and misery.

One day we will realize that the origin of injustice in the world is the belief in Karma based on good and evil. On that day, all these fanaticisms will become dark memories and history.

I tell you decisively, the ugliest, most ignorant, worst, and most hated people in the world are valuable like me and anyone else in the world.

If there are such undeveloped people in the world, it is because of their own limited emotions and thoughts and the irresponsibility of them and us.

All of us must be ashamed of having such people.

My suggestion for the treatment of ugliness, ignorance, and evil is only strengthening the manifestation of beauty, knowledge, perception, and goodness unconditionally.

It is the extract of the training of great people like Gandhi and Martin Luther King.

33

Is the comparison correct if we say that crystal is weaker and less valuable, and that steel is more powerful and more valuable? Of course, I prefer none of them, but a diamond!

In the same way, the human characteristics of women and men are different, and they are not comparable.

Men and women, in the path of transcendence, need to be able to understand each other well as human beings and divine creatures.

Femininity and masculinity are traits of human society.

I am not talking about the variable and relative laws of human society.

I am talking about the global law in which male superiority is meaningless in it.

Even transgender people are valuable in the same way as other men and women. Also, they can be among the world's greatest spiritual leaders.

The truth and oneness of your existence are like a diamond and beyond any gender and sexuality.

In the past, my thoughts and feelings were minimal, and I believed they were the absolute truth.

Years ago, I thought that the unity of humanity and the world was meaningless.

Years later, I realized that my past thoughts and feelings were meaningless. I was blind, deaf, and insensitive at that time, and I could not understand love and the oneness.

After years of research and experience, I thought I was a thinker and emotional, but later I realized that my thoughts and emotions are minimal, and none of them are the truth.

An ordinary human being cannot understand his/her existence, which is part of the oneness, on the basis that he/she thinks that his/her thoughts, feelings, and beliefs are the absolute truth.

A normal person cannot move well on the path to success and transcendence because she/he places her/his life based on her/his or others' beliefs and imaginary values, not the realities of the world.

A great human being can understand that the truth is beyond his/her feelings, thoughts, and beliefs, and can understand the oneness in the path to the development of his/her mind and heart.

A great human being can move on the path to success and transcendence because she/he lives based on global laws and realities.

36

Fake great men and women are the rulers of others' ego. They temporarily change the appearance of the world.

Ordinary humans are obedient to others' ego. They keep the current conditions of the world.

Successful humans are obedient to their egos. These are theoreticians of a different and new world.

Great human beings are the rulers of their ego. They are the model and the creator of a new and better world.

37

In ordinary societies, many social laws and values are created by a few people and based on old beliefs and imposed on the entire community.

In a love-based society, the true values of everyone are discovered, flourished, and strengthened by unifying personal values of individuals based on their diverse interests and abilities, dynamic and live social laws, and values will be manifested.

38

Some of us have learned to believe that mental, emotional, physical boundaries and bias toward special people or something is sacred and represented as love.

Such a fake love makes us hate others, the human community to be fragmented, and in certain circumstances, even crimes can be considered permissible and proud.

This is a pseudo-spirituality. This is a mental deception.

If I think that my thoughts, feelings, and beliefs are more valuable than others', I am totally mistaken and misled.

Based on true love and spirituality, you unconsciously respect all human beings, creatures, and the world.

True unconditional love shines like the sun to all human beings and creatures of the world.

39

If one person is a negative person, but he/she genuinely believes that he/she is a good person, his/her appearance will be humanitarian.

You usually cannot understand if such a person is truly a good person or not.

40

In a healthy society, more valuable human beings are those who have more open minds and deeper feelings to themselves, others, and the whole universe, not those who have more wealth and power.

41

Fortunately, the Universal Declaration of Human Rights (UDHR) is a declaration adopted by the United Nations on December 10, 1948.

Unfortunately, we have deceived ourselves for a long time because we still have not accepted all people of the world as human beings who have the same human rights.

No matter what, some people are like slaves or will be killed because we think this is based on their KARMA, not our irresponsibility!

Your love is just self-deception if you cannot believe in the oneness of humanity and the collective global KARMA.

42

The suffering of many of those who suffer in the world is not due to something called personal Karma, but their plight is based on inefficient political, economic, and military systems that are based on global Karma.

The prevailing global Karma is what proves the whole of humanity and the universe is one, and it is possible that I could be hurt here because of the mistake of another person or other people at another point in the world.

We think that these are just incidental, but there is nothing accidental in the world, and all the events are based on our common global karma.

43

If some people in different parts of the world are plagued or killed, this is not based on secret divine wisdom to sacrifice innocent people.

Rather, it is based on our ignorance and irresponsibility that we abuse concepts such as God, wisdom, Karma, love, and philanthropy in our interest to the detriment of weak people.

44

The people who have lost the true meaning of their life and have built their lives based on the suggested social values, cannot understand their connection with other creatures and humans.

45

Most of the problems in our world are based on ignorance, irresponsibility, and sanctification of our thoughts, feelings, and beliefs, not the lack of facilities on the planet earth and natural disasters.

46

In the world, there are great human beings who care about love and philanthropy more than their financial, personal, and group interests. This is a matter of relaxing the hearts and minds of the people who hope for the manifestation of a better and more beautiful world.

These great human beings are the people who have kept the dignity of humanity; otherwise, with the vast ignorance and irresponsibility of the human community against major crimes based on economic, political, and military systems, I would not prefer to be a human being.

47

There is nothing quite the same in nature.

Two identical robots can be produced artificially, but there can never be two completely similar trees in nature.

None of us are equal, but each one of us is a unique being. At the same time, we have the right to choose equality for the creation of our lives based on our talents and our abilities.

We do not need to be equal like robots, but each one of us must try to be a global leader in terms of his/her unique talents and abilities.

48

The belief that my family and I are more valuable than others, and if necessary, the interests of others must be sacrificed for my family and me is one of the most dangerous mental viruses in human society.

One who has such a belief will never be able to love others unconditionally.

My family and I are not more valuable than others, but our success and transcendence take priority so that we can be like a pillar for the success and transcendence of others and the human community. All together, we create a world that is better and more just for my family and me.

49

From childhood, our subconscious mind is programmed by indirect suggestions of parents and our community. A significant part of our inner world is built based on the same recommendations.

If we cannot be able to change our inner world and make it better and more beautiful, our lives will be in vain.

50

Having the same wealth and capabilities which others have does not matter.

What matters is the equal right to choose and the opportunity to try to earn the things that matter to us, not to anyone else.

51

People need equal rights to choose, not equal facilities and conditions.

52

Freedom is not a gift that powerful people give to weak people.

Freedom means respect for the "equal right to choose" one another as human beings who each one is a massive world and a model of an infinite unity of the universe.

Such freedom is based on the freedom and tranquility of our personal inner world.

Ultimately, our free inner worlds can come together in the depths of our existence, and true love, freedom, and peace manifest in the physical world.

53

I do not say anything you would like or believe, but something that is the truth of my inner world.

It seems that the system of slavery has ended for many years, but this is not true.

This system has been more advanced and subtle. In a way that you think you are free, but at the same time, you are under the control of political and economic systems.

This freedom is a mirage, and unconditional love cannot be based on the illusion.

You can love unconditionally when in the depths of your heart and soul, you can feel that you are free like a God, not while the political and economic systems are your true God.

Those who look for the truth, they can understand that there is neither border between the physical and spiritual worlds nor between you and the Gods.

There is the oneness, and its divine power is an unconditional love that needs to be manifested in our heart, soul, and society. Then we will be able to understand who we are and how we've been able to live and proud of our humiliation under the political and economic systems.

After that, we will understand that these systems were established based on a world full of violence and selfishness, and then you will know what the real change will be.

54

Global human rights and love under political and economic systems are merely a dead body and seductive instrument.

55

Nowadays, political, and economic systems are real God in the world, and not the God of religions.

Even religious people are a slave to these systems, but they are unaware or do not want to believe it because they do not like other people knowing that everything is just a professional show.

All these mental games are valuable, and even sacred to you unless you let your ego and beliefs fade, and you see the real values in the light of true love.

56

In a loving relationship between two healthy people, you will try to improve an imperfect relationship based on the art of living and loving, when true love shines from your heart and soul.

Otherwise, you'll try to run away from your problems and change your partners, while in this way your problems can be more and worse.

Do you know why?

First, only a true and pure love can let us be patient and strong enough to learn the art of living and loving.

Second, you can only have a superficial relationship because you will have to hide most problems from new partners if you change your partner regularly. Therefore, you will never have the opportunity to recognize the issues and to find solutions.

Also, you will not be able to love unconditionally because you will not have the ability to change yourself in the path of actual growth and transcendence, but only changing your partners like your clothes.

Pure and unconditional love is the art of those who want to change themselves to experience a better relationship, not the people who try to change others to find the perfect man/woman who doesn't like to be like them.

57

The biggest problem and the inner obstacle in our life for change and transformation is our lack of confidence, a defect of faith, and also the lack of assurance regarding the wiping out of the past and the negative points of our life to replace them with a life based on goodness and truth.

Most people maybe want to change and transform themselves; however, because of the lack of guarantees and lack of real practical models, they cannot go forward in this path. Few people are willing to take risks and take cautious steps.

In fact, the overwhelming majority of people in the community are less likely to take risks because of many and successive failures in many small and large issues. This is the greatest risk in life that causes the change and transformation of all the existence of someone.

All are afraid that their whole lives would probably fall apart, and they do not get what they wanted. Also, they are afraid if they fail, they will even lose the way back to their previous lives.

58

Ordinary marriage is a complete mental and physical relationship that both parties may have emotional and spiritual connections. In other words, in terms of physical and bodily contact, they may be committed to each other, but their hearts and souls have no obligation to each other -- even if they do not express it supposedly.

True marriage is a pure relationship between two hearts and souls that both parties have physical connections. In other words, their hearts and souls are committed to each other, and, consequently, they will be physically committed to each other even if they do not express it.

59

In a dictatorship society, the most significant pain of a free-minded person is when his/her home is a jail.

She/he, despite having many talents and abilities, cannot be helpful, and while each knows, thinks, and feels, must live like someone who does not exist at all.

The most painful thing is when one cannot even talk about it while speaking.

60

Those who sacrifice their love, whether their beloved, their talents and their interests, for transient benefits, money, sex, and power, put a stain of shame on humanity's face and enslave themselves and the human community by spreading the oppression and injustice in the world.

61

Those who sell their bodies do not lead society to degeneracy, but those who sell their hearts and souls make human society corrupt and devastated and spoil the face of humanity.

62

Always try to choose love and peace, not war.

However, sometimes there are situations that you want to choose love and peace, but you cannot.

In such situations, try to fight to protect justice, love, and peace, and not to destroy the people, or their belongings.

63

If there are poor people and we think it is not justice to see them like this, then we should help them to have their income, or share our profits with them individually or collectively.

Otherwise, it is not pure goodness, but self-deception if we give them a little food, etc., to make them satisfied like animals.

64

Fake goodness is offering something that does not affect your life and something you do not care about.

True goodness is giving something that affects your life and something you care about.

65

A nation that only sees black and white, how can it not have color blindness and see the color of happiness? It comes from the same religious culture that says one is perfectly good and holy, and anyone else is always bad and evil. The culture, which derived from religion, has taken power from us to see other colors except for black and white.

66

The biggest dilemmas and injustices in the world are due to the politics of the people who have power but do not understand humanitarian principles.

67

Under the name of religion and God, we can cover every crime with the words of sacred and divine, and we close our eyes to wisdom, logic, dignity, and humanitarian principles.

68

Most of the time, there is no real and fundamental problem between lovers, but because of the ignorance of one or both sides, a minor problem becomes so essential that the whole relationship breaks down.

For simple food, we learn how to eat it properly.

However, our culture and the teaching of our communication relationships are so weak that people may not pass any training for a relationship, love expression, and lovemaking, etc., which have the most significant role in a person's life. They think it is enough to know and hear sporadic and non-scientific information and in the same way, a miracle happens, they fall in love with each other, expect another miracle and experience the best and joyful life and happiness together.

69

Before we have any particular religion, race, or nationality, we are all human beings, and that is what matters first.

Unfortunately, human societies are so full of people with low IQs that they do not understand this undeniable fact. They measure the quality of a human being according to their religion, race, and nationality, and based on that, they interpret human rights to the same extent that your humanity, according to religion, race, and nationality, is confirmed. Thus, surmising that you will be able to enjoy the same amount of human rights. The Universal Declaration of Human Rights regarded the recognition of equal rights of human beings unconditionally, and regardless of their religion, race, and nationality. However, there is still no country in the world where your humanity has priority, and your human rights will be recognized unconditionally, except in the South Pole!

70

In a dictatorship society, there is no need to fight the dictators who are well-diggers at the bottom of the well.

The greatest weakness of dictators is the values of the dictatorship in the society, not political and military forces.

The only way is to break down dictatorial values from the society that are the pillars of the dictatorial system.

It needs a social evolution for fundamental change and democratization, and not a political reform or revolution to beautify the dictatorial community.

71

Democracy began from the people's thought and heart and culture, not merely social and political apparent changes.

72

True marriage means a bond between two people based on unconditional love on the path of emotional and spiritual unity, even if they are different physically and intellectually.

A marriage based on financial and social benefits and with a commitment on a paper, not in the depths of our souls and hearts, is a business deal and a fleeting joy. This is all about an emotional business plan to have someone or something and to get more.

True love is not about having business with body, heart, and soul to get more, but it is about being better and giving more by heart, soul, and body. When it is mutual and unconditional between two people, it is a true marriage, nothing more.

Political and religious systems do not recognize true marriage because they fear to be questioned about their values and economic benefits.

73

The political boundaries of the world should be opened unconditionally to all human beings respecting human rights.

Restricting people based on their place of birth and financial status is the result of the management of immature people who exploit universal human rights for personal and regional and economic interests.

Before we can unconditionally love each other, all of us must have the right to choose equality in the world. Otherwise, your path and my path to unconditional love are wrong.

74

One of the most important obstacles to the realization of human rights in the world is monetary policy and the economic system based on monetary values and the common economic needs of democratic and non-democratic countries to each other.

75

Imposing the husband's surname on the wife is based on the old patriarchal culture when a woman was considered a property of a man, which should be recorded in his name.

The man should not have any superior position, but both must have equal rights to choose. They can have a mutual decision about a common surname for each other and for their children.

76

We are all divine creatures whose common points are much more and more profound than some of the apparent differences.

Hiding this truth and dividing between people is only in the interests of corrupt political, economic, and belief systems for the brainwashing of human beings. They try to make us believe in each other's false despicableness to highlight differences artificially. This is the root and foundation of a long-term plan to control people by those systems to ensure the security of their interests.

Freeness out of the Systems

77

The political borders among countries and humans are just a falsehood and are imposed by low-minded people.

It is enough to deepen our hearts and mind; then, we will be embarrassed about how we could believe the false borders between humans and even call it holy, and therefore oppress some regions (means countries) of the united world and allow crime for them.

78

It is wrong if we expect people to get more money if they have more in-depth thoughts and a greater spirit.

Like fictitious boundaries between humans, money, and monetary credits, not material facilities, are illusional values, and that is not compatible with the spirit of philanthropy.

Of course, the benefits of having more and better services and facilities are not conflicting with the quality of thought and spirit of a person, but it is not understandable based on monetary valuation. That's why the problem, without solving, is cleared on this basis by the monetary valuation; and practically, the distinction between superior thoughts and spirit is impossible and often worthless according to the monetary valuation.

We can strive to provide facilities and services according to thoughts and emotions, instead of expecting that our ideas and spirit be valued based on monetary credits.

79

Two major obstacles for the transcendence of human societies are the "political boundaries among countries and regions," and "valuing everything and every one based on monetary credits."

80

The without borders virtual community, on the *Web* and the *Internet*, is the best model to create an international community without the political boundaries.

Believing in political borders is a hallucination.

Since childhood, by parents and society, we have been hypnotized and conditioned to believe that this hallucination is the reality.

We do not need any sovereign and border on the world; we only need experts on the different fields to be society observers and not to be involved in the various issues to limit others based on certain beliefs.

81

The lives of humans are sacred, not the differences and boundaries between humans.

The borders of the countries of the world were different in the past. Hundreds of millions of people were killed and made the current form.

Based on believing in the boundaries of countries, of course, people will try to broaden or break up countries in the future, which would also kill hundreds of millions of other people.

The problem between Palestine and Israel, and so on, will not be resolved until the moment we do not have the wisdom and awareness to understand that the differences and boundaries between humans are not sacred, but the lives of humans are.

82

We cannot destroy the political borders by force.

We can try to make each country a region which all together can become the United States of the World.

If we can develop a global love culture in the world, the political borders between humans will fade gradually.

83

There are no boundaries other than natural barriers.

This is our limited thoughts and feelings that have made distance among humankind and have separated humans.

84

A world without borders can be manifested with creating a new civilization based on international and natural values at the height of technology and social progress.

85

The world and its possibilities belong to all the people on the planet.

Making limitations for some nations and individuals in certain parts of the world is human rights violations and an insult to humanity.

86

The people who are humans, the same way we are, do not have the right to stop us in a particular area of the world and to control our lives.

87

Economic values are based on our separation, and humanitarian values are based on love and unity.

In a world where economic values are more important than human values, we can be friends with each other, but we can never genuinely love each other.

We need new and better valuation criteria.

The significant problems of human society can be solved only when the economic values adequately serve humanitarian values.

88

Judging humans based on their place of birth and financial ability means ridiculing universal human rights and human values.

Universal human rights and unconditional love will only be a theory and cannot be realized, while false economic criteria and political borders can separate us from each other.

Those who believe, based on the current political and economic systems, it is possible to manifest universal human rights and true unconditional love, they are plunged into delusion.

89

It is impossible for anyone to love you unconditionally when his/her life is dependent on the economic system.

90

An economic genius is not one who is millions of times more intelligent and more valuable than others. Services, talents, and abilities of some other people are not so worthless that they die of hunger with such an advanced and sophisticated brain!

The main problem is not people who do not want a good life, but a corrupt economic system.

The world's economic system has been developed based on old and wrong criteria.

In this system, incomparable things are compared to each other. For example, how could one kilo of fruit have the same value as a book?

Also, in this system, many valuable things are known as worthless things and vice versa.

The economic system is a one-dimensional and limited system for valuation. While the actual value of a variety of things is remarkably diverse, we need a multi-dimensional method to evaluate them.

91

Normally, the services of some people are thousands of times more important than many people, but there is not a single person whom her/his services and work is not worth a little food, medicine, and simple needs.

It is a disgrace to the human race that the economic system allows many members of our global family to suffer or lose their lives only for a small amount of food and medicine.

Unconditional love is not just a little affection for each other, as civilized slaves, but an attempt to find a better alternative to wrong systems and to strengthen new values in human society.

92

Only the natural boundaries of the world are real, and the political boundaries are the result of limited minds and hearts of our ancestors.

In the current world, most of the boundaries of communication have disappeared, and the division among humans is unfortunate in the vast universe on which planet earth has nothing in it.

In this age, we take pride in this fanaticism and ignorance, but one day our posterity will laugh at it.

The political and economic systems have limited our minds and hearts like unbelievably cheap creatures for a small part of the planet. This is a suggested and illusional reality by family and society.

You are like a god/goddess that all the universe can belong to you, and in the future, even the boundary among the planets of the solar system may become meaningless for us - - this is the reality of ours and the world.

93

There are no pure and unconditional human rights in this world.

In democratic countries, you should be a citizen, and then you will be recognized as a human being who has legal and social rights.

In dictatorial countries, you should be obedient and slave, and then you will be recognized as an ignorant child who has legal and social rights but under the supervision of the dictators as wise parents.

There is a third group of people who believe it is not the political borders or systems that determine their identity, but those who they indeed are within and what they think, feel, and do for flourishing and transcendence of humanity.

94

A system of slavery determines how much you are valuable, how much you can be free, and how much you have the right to choose.

We now have three types of modern slavery systems.

The first kind of slavery system is local, and you can see in dictatorial countries.

This is political, social, and religious slavery; however, most of the people have grown with such slavery in a way that some people have believed that it is holy and valuable. They think that is the maximum freedom that they must have, and they imagine the things others imposed on them are their own choices.

The second slavery system is political in different countries but more democratic.

This is political slavery, and the governments can play with the whole lives of many people whom most of them escaped from the first slavery system. They have the name of "asylum-seekers" in the second slavery system, and the political interests of governments determine to allow them to be free and have the right to choose or decide about their lives like animals.

The third modern slavery system is global and around the World. This is the most advanced system of slavery throughout human history when the monetary system determines how much you are valuable, how much you can be free, and how much you have the right to choose. However, billions of people around the world are in this illusion that they are entirely free with equal rights to choose.

We believe that this system is the solution to most human problems, and we do not want to wake up and see that it is the cause of the biggest dilemmas of human society.

95

I hope that one day, this false political borders and lineation among humans will disappear, which is the result of the racist stupidity of people in ancient times.

96

There is no doubt that we need the ability to get what we need; however, money is a wrong valuation tool for products and also for human beings in a way that splits human beings and prevents them from having the ability to love each other unconditionally. Religious systems also trade their beliefs with money, and if they do not have money, they will lose most of their power.

Your Loveliness

97

Love is not limited to one person or a certain number of people.

Infatuation toward one person or certain people or a particular nation, while at the same time belittling others and even having feelings of hatred toward others, is something like racism and cannot be love, but pseudo-love.

True love manifests based on self-awareness of unity and oneness.

98

The city and country of a lover is the entire width of the planet earth, and each human being is a member of her/his global family.

99

True love is magnificent, but it is only a stage which with understanding and immersing in it, we will be able to understand and experience extraordinary and higher stages.

This is the nature of the world that there may always be something better, and at the same time, the best thing in the world is still unknown.

100

If we read hundreds of thousands of books, if we experience hundreds of thousands of pleasures and pain, we finally find that life is absurd.

When we understand the true love, we realize that the only thing that is truly worthy is the expression of love and helping each other unconditionally.

101

I do not like anyone's ignorance and dirtiness, prejudice, racism, ugliness, and immoral behavior. However, I and others, apart from all the problems and shortcomings, are all part of the oneness and deserve unconditional love and acceptance of each other.

102

Unconditional love is not just a good feeling toward oneself and others, but it is the root of an advanced and practical culture based on human rights and philanthropy and common humanitarian values.

103

Any idea that causes humans to confront humans and considers differences as more important than common human values is incorrect.

Enmity, war, to be killed and killing other people in any way, do not have any honor to me.

War and killing are caused by ignorance and illusion of humans, which is the heritage of wild animals, not the fruit of human civilization.

The culmination of human understanding and civilization is the unity and love and respecting for human rights of the whole humanity unconditionally (and beyond economic interests).

The shortcomings and issues of the world, whether directly or indirectly, are the result of wrongful thoughts, feelings, and acts or indifference of all of us in the past and now.

104

If there are more complex issues, their solution is not inattention to them, but we must work harder and more to reach their answer.

Successful people in critical situations try to solve the issues better and more, and in optimal conditions, they work to accept more responsibilities.

If human beings have not yet succeeded in accepting a without borders world based on love and philanthropy, or if we live in hatred and constraints, the solution is not inattention to this issue.

We must work harder to find solutions to these problems and to create a world without borders based on love and philanthropy.

The solution to hate and intense hostility between people is a massive and unconditional love manifestation.

105

Without enough knowledge, understanding, and practice, we cannot love unconditionally.

For example, most of the words of a philosophical book may be familiar to us, but we cannot understand and explain the subject of the book. Why? Because we have to have specialist knowledge of philosophy to understand philosophical issues.

Only in such a situation, we can be a philosopher and distinguish between fallacy and philosophy.

Similarly, romantic, and humanitarian words and sentences may be familiar to us, but maybe we are not able to understand and practice them. Why? Because to understand the oneness and unconditional love, we require a profound and specialist knowledge and understanding of the unity of humans and creatures.

With such an understanding, we can love unconditionally and distinguish between unconditional love and conditional love.

Just as becoming a philosopher or loving unconditionally is the result of perception and expertise, fallacy or conditional love may look very real like playing a professional actor, but it is the result of a lack of understanding and knowledge in philosophy or true love.

Unconditional love is not a show, but a kind of culture and way of life.

106

Unconditional love is not weakness and ignorance but is based on an intuitive understanding, wisdom, and power which manifests our inner harmony and beauty.

Imagine an incredibly beautiful woman who has many charms for most men and even women. Such an attraction is the result of her fit body and behavior.

Without any effort, the charm is a part of her naturalness. In fact, this attraction is valuable and widely considered by others because it is natural and not fabricated.

When the inner understanding and wisdom of a human being becomes so dominant in a way that it erupts as true love, such a love reflects the harmony, beauty, and unity of his/her inner world within and brings out the charm that is a real part of her/his existence.

Under such conditions, loving unconditionally will be one of the most natural human behaviors. Whenever naturally and like breathing, our behavior towards friends and enemies is based on love and philanthropy, then our love is unconditional.

If someone is currently unable to love others unconditionally, pretending will be an obstacle for his/her growth and transcendence.

One of the hallmarks of conditional love is arrogance, not self-esteem, and self-confidence.

As eating is a natural need and cannot be the reason for our arrogance, the same way, loving others unconditionally is our own natural need. This is a pleasure, euphoria, and the best gift.

Understanding of oneness and uniqueness makes such greatness within us that even thinking about having arrogance in front of others is childish and ridiculous.

Unlocking our minds and feelings for diverse types of knowledge, cultures, and beliefs, and usual critiquing and reformation of our minds and emotions can lead our growth and transcendence path to the unconditional love.

Several principles of unconditional love are as follows:

1. I cannot always know many things.

2. I can always make mistakes about what I know.

3. I can always learn more and better things from others.

4. The power of unconditional love comes from the power of inner understanding and wisdom.

5. The desire to love unconditionally manifests as one of the vital human needs and behaviors not as an outward appearance of humanitarian behaviors.

107

In our inner world, there are many thoughts, feelings, and beliefs.

The inner world of each one of us, like the physical world, is very complex and varied.

When some of our thoughts and feelings are suppressed or neglected, some inner inconsistency arises that harms our lives.

To achieve peace and growth and transcendence of our personality and lives, we must allow all kinds of thoughts and feelings to emerge.

Unconditional love is based on unconditional inner freedom of expression and respect for inner different and even contradictory thoughts and feelings and beliefs.

When peace and tranquility are created among different characters in our inner world, our path will be ready to love our various internal and outer aspects unconditionally.

This is the starting point to love others unconditionally.

If we are unconcerned to some people in the world or we suppress some thoughts and feelings of others, it reflects the existence of irresponsibility or repression in our inner world. Under such conditions, unconditional love for oneself and others is a mirage.

When we are unable to establish peace in our inner world, under normal circumstances, we move unconsciously on our gradual suicide, and we commit murder and crimes under very critical circumstances.

Hostility, war and crime, the inconsistency of nations, followers of different religions and beliefs, and a life based on the belief in our separation from each other, is a kind of culture for gradually and unconsciously destroying our original identity and our authentic lives. The authentic life is far beyond only being alive.

Unconditional love for oneself and others is based on the recognition of distinct aspects of the inner world and the understanding and acceptance of inner freedom and unity.

When someone can love herself/himself and others unconditionally, she/he may have very different thoughts, feelings, and behaviors, but there is a kind of harmony and unity among them.

108

We may think, feel, and believe for better or for worse.

What are our thoughts, feelings, and beliefs?

They are the creator of the unconscious mind and our inner world.

Have we built our inner world after discovering the truth? No!

We have created this world based on the words and behaviors of others and our imaginations.

This world may be the masterpiece of the creation of our lives, but it is not a place to discover the absolute truth.

When we uncover the boundaries of our thoughts, feelings, and beliefs, in other words, our inner world connects itself to the inner worlds of other individuals and creatures; we reach a stage where we can be free from the limitation of specific thoughts, feelings, and beliefs. For instance, a spacecraft that is released from gravity can move about in an exceedingly massive and infinite world.

The secret of our transcendence is based on the liberation from the shackles of the inner world.

In such a situation, we can understand the oneness and unconditional love beyond fictional worlds of ourselves and others and beyond the words and the imaginations that we now have in our minds.

The truth manifests in the path of collective wisdom and the collective unconscious.

It is better to stop if we accepted the beliefs that distract us from understanding our unity and unconditional love because it is a sign that we are lost in an infinite false inner world, but we think we are on the right path. A world that looks very real but achieving the truth in it will be nothing more than a mirage.

The first step in the path of unconditional love is to face and embrace the inner worlds of oneself and others with all the ugly and beautiful characters inside.

109

Where is the boundary of unconditional love for others? Is it only with our thoughts, feelings, behavior, and speech? Or, also, with the body and sexual relations?

Is it right to show unconditional love with sex and body addition to verbal and behavioral love, with many people you like, and you want?

It depends on you and the other party. You have the right to choose. If you think it is right, you can select it; otherwise, you do not have to accept such a thing.

We do not have the right to impose a particular way on anyone.

In any case, unconditional love is a divine act, and in the same way that our thoughts, feelings, behavior, and speech can be divine, our physical and sexual relationships can also turn into sacred lovemaking.

110

When you love your family or friends, your love is not based on their appearance, wealth, position, and knowledge.

Unconditional love means that all the other people, regardless of whether they are wealthy or poor, powerful or weak, ignorant or scientist, etc., can all be part of our family.

To become a great man or woman, we need to open our hearts and minds.

When we realize that our family members and our home are in distinct parts of the world, we experience the most beautiful feeling of the world, and that is nothing but happiness.

111

Under normal circumstances, we have confined ourselves to solid mental and emotional fences, and we cannot have a deeply passionate and romantic relationship with different and unknown people.

As we expand our thoughts and feelings, we can establish deep and sincere relationships with more humans.

The one who has a great goal, bravely steps in, even in the middle of the darkness of the night, ruggedly and dangerously, until finally reaches her/his goal.

Unconditional love is like that. Unconditional love means going into the unknown worlds of others at the height of courage and companionship and communication with the heart and soul of human beings on the path of growth and transcendence.

By gaining knowledge and wealth, you can be a successful person, but if you want to be a great human being, your path does not go through the facilities and different things, but the path of your growth and transcendence goes straight from the heart and soul of human beings.

112

In normal circumstances, the various aspects of your inner world are confronting each other.

When you can manage peace and calmness in your inner world, you can quickly and unconditionally love yourself.

And when you can understand and coordinate the relationships between your inner world and the physical world, unconditional love for the living beings will be a natural part of your existence.

Ultimately, you will be able to understand the unity among your existence and humanity and the universe.

At this point, you are free from the shackles of the mind, time, and being, and at the actual present moment, you will understand the living and inexpressible masterpieces of the world.

This understanding is what you need to become a great man or woman. You do not need to take any other actions, because you automatically and naturally live like a great human, and you will not be anyone except your true self who is a great human being.

The inner masculine part of you is the creator of the masterpieces of the world, and the inner feminine piece is the heart and soul and life-giving part of the world masterpieces.

When these two parts of your existence fall in love with each other, and they reach unity, you can unconditionally love yourself and others.

Being in love with yourself and others, unconditionally, means inner celebration, dance, and happiness at the height of your privacy, uniqueness, and greatness.

Maybe all humans cannot be beautiful, but all humans can be attractive and lovely with their unconditional love for themselves and others.

No matter if you are beautiful or not, If the deepest layers of your existence accept unconditional love, your physical appearance will change as well. You may not be beautiful, but the charm of your being will be much more valuable than ordinary beauty.

Having beautiful thoughts and feelings is much more important than apparent beauty.

The secret of inner greatness is to create a beautiful inner world where beautiful thoughts and emotions grow and erupt in the physical world.

115

You can quickly love the rich, perfect, healthy, wise, powerful, beautiful, and ideal people. Such love is conditional.

Unconditional love to the poor, incomplete, sick, ignorant, weak, and ugly people is essential.

I do not mean acceptance and confirmation of poverty, deficiency, disease, ignorance, weakness, and ugliness.

Unconditional love means we accept unconditionally other human beings so that they can grow.

Under such conditions, cheap personalities become valued personalities. And valuable people become more valuable people.

Unconditional love is the art of manifestation, growth, and transcendence of the ideals of ourselves and others.

116

If two people want to have an ideal life together and move in peace and happiness along the path of progress and transcendence, they must try to:

 - Unconditionally get connected and acquainted with various aspects of each other; physically, mentally, emotionally, and spiritually.

 - Forget about their gender and embrace their uniqueness and unity beyond femininity and masculinity.

117

The only thing that can make our lives meaningful in every situation and every day is to love the heart and soul and lovely existence of other human beings and creatures directly and unconditionally.

If someone is in love with you, he/she may give you many things, but if millions of people in the world love you, your path to realizing great goals will be smooth.

You have one choice to achieve lofty goals -- lead your talents and abilities and interests unconditionally and unlimitedly in the path of true love and philanthropy to other human beings and creatures.

118

If you truly love someone, you are ready to sacrifice your whole existence and life for her/him.

Also, if you genuinely love other humans and creatures unconditionally, you will sacrifice your past thoughts and feelings and beliefs for global interests. The selfishness of ego disappears, and greatness and beauty and the unity of the universe are manifested in your being.

119

The first lessons of unconditional love are:

- I am willing to sacrifice my interests for the sake of the unity of the world and not the interests of others.

- I am ready to expand my mind and feelings to connect with your heart and soul.

- It does not matter to me if you are my enemy or my friend or if you are beneficial for me. In any case, you are part of my oneness that I love with my whole being.

120

You may know how it feels to love someone so much to the depth of your soul. Oh, it's very nice.

However, unconditional love is about a global romantic and divine relationship and coordination when our soul is in love with billions of people and other creatures.

True love between two people is precious; nevertheless, the perception of oneness is billions of times more enjoyable than ordinary love.

This is our most important need. This is inexpressible, featureless, and inconceivable. This is unconditional love.

121

True love is the only specialized language in the world that even illiterate and immature people understand it to its fullest.

If you are a scientist or wise, only professionals or intellectuals can understand your words when you speak in layman's terms, but if you are a manifestation of oneness and your teachings erupt with the genuine unconditional love from your existence, the majority of people will understand your words.

122

The clouds of ignorance and prejudice and hatred may temporarily hide the sky and the sun of love and awareness, but in all circumstances, our oneness will remain unchanged.

Try to manifest the infinite source of love within you, and like the sun, share the light and heat of love to yourself, other human beings, and creatures.

This source of love is not one person, but our oneness.

Hate and ignorance are our ego's shadows. When we can understand unity; the ego and its shadow disappear, and then the light and warmth of the sun of love and awareness will cover all our lives and our world; we will witness the birth of a new world.

The world we love each other as part of our unity with our whole hearts and souls.

123

No language or words can express an inexplicable truth.

Unconditional love for ugly and beautiful humans and creatures is the only indirect, valid, and universal language for the manifestation of the truth and oneness on this planet.

When you can understand unconditional love, you will realize that all physical and spiritual boundaries of the world are children's Jokes and subjective deceptions.

The truth and true love have no boundaries, not even extensive borders.

124

When you are original, and like a hollow flute, then part of the oneness can flow into your existence and manifest as the melody of unconditional love in the world.

125

Conditional love is dependent on our minds and our emotions. We try to keep it alive, but surely it will die. We are striving to carry its rotten corpse, but it is dead forever, and our heart is numb with it.

But true unconditional love is beyond our existence. Our minds and emotions die in true love at any moment and are reborn again. True love is equal to eternal freshness and eternal life at "The present moment."

126

True love is a global power that binds us as parts of the oneness.

127

Conditional love can only be part of our behavior, speech, or belief. These are just masks and dummy shows.

When true and unconditional love is part of our identity, our existence, and our lives, we witness something that is our real face.

128

When you open the gates of your heart and soul, ugliness and beauty, suffering, and pleasure simultaneously cover your existence.

Someone who can love unconditionally, his/her sensitivity significantly increases to all good, bad, and even very trivial things, but at the same time, her/his capacity and the power of tolerance and acceptance of diversity and differences are also significantly increased.

When you can cross the borders of Hell and paradise, then you can love freely and unconditionally.

129

You can genuinely be in love with another person if you are able to love yourself, human beings, and creatures.

Otherwise, your love is an illusion if you cannot love yourself and people unconditionally.

130

If your love leads you to an understanding of our unity, it is true; otherwise, it is a mirage.

131

Conditional love is like a beautiful crystal that can easily break.

Unconditional love is like a diamond that is beautiful and very resistant.

If our love is fragile and unstable and it undermines our character, it's better to break it because this is a fake thing.

True love manifests as part of our essence and existence, and it is so powerful that it transforms us into international geniuses and great men and women.

Do not be in the shackles of fake love. Sometimes, after hundreds of times breaking fake love, true love can emerge in our existence.

Of course, if you cannot experience fake love, you will most likely never be able to understand true love.

132

Love is the only power that makes us realize that our existence and unity are more than all thoughts, beliefs, and ideologies -- without exception.

133

Love is not only the expression of feelings but the most magnificent art piece in your life.

If you learn this amazing art, your life and romance will ultimately become a masterpiece of the world.

Love is like a lovely baby who is born shortly, but not perfect.

Just like raising a child, we must learn the art of life and romantic relationships better and better so that this incredible power of our existence evolves and becomes mature.

If you cannot learn the art of romantic relationships with yourself and another human being, you will never be able to learn the art of unconditional love for billions of humans and other creatures.

134

According to economic and political systems, only our separation is meaningful, and true love and oneness are stupid things.

There is no way but only to be free from the slavery of these systems; otherwise, you can never be able to love unconditionally.

135

No matter if I can, or cannot, in any case, I breathe, even in the worst circumstances.

In the case of love, this is the same.

No matter what situation and what limitations you have, and no matter who your beloved is, in any case, you love her/him because love is part of your existence, and without it, your life will become meaningless.

This love is unconditional.

If your beloved's behaviors, your problems, or environmental conditions can reduce or eliminate your love, you still have not learned the art of unconditional love, and your love is either imperfect or fake.

The laws of love are contradictory to economic rules. Do not expect any rewards in the future.

When your love alone is the reward of your love, and the roots of your love are in the depths of your heart and soul, not your beloved, then your love is true, and you have learned the first lesson of the art of unconditional love.

136

In the depths of our existence, based on unity, we are all in touch with each other.

Love the unique soul in the depths of your beloved's existence, not just his/her behaviors and words.

In such circumstances, it does not matter whether he/she is leaving you, because in any case, you like him/her as part of your united existence.

If you cannot love someone who has left you, you will never be able to love others unconditionally.

It's not easy, but it's a measure to make sure your love is true or not.

In any case, this power of your inner love will make your heart and soul clearer in the path of transcendence and success, and as a result, you will become someone who can easily penetrate deep into the hearts and minds of humans.

In other words, you will become known as a symbol of the unity of the depth of existence of human beings and creatures. You will become someone who based on a deep understanding of oneness, can be an immensely helpful person for herself/himself, other human beings, and creatures.

And the secret of the meaning of life lies in unconditional love and being helpful based on your interests, talents, and abilities.

137

I wish we could develop unconditional love in the world with positive words, but these only have superficial effects.

We can love practically and unconditionally when economic, political, and military systems do not enslave our lives.

If we cannot sacrifice our economic interests for the sake of love and philanthropy, our positive thoughts are self-deceptive.

138

For those who truly and unconditionally love, a cosmic force erupts from their existence that can penetrate deep into the hearts and souls of others.

75

In other words, the existence of such people unconsciously makes the harmony and bond between individuals and beings stronger, and our unity begins to manifest.

139

This is our most significant mistake in life if love is in our minds, but not in our hearts and hands.

This mental love is the best way to get more ego benefits, and an illusion and self-deception, and the most significant way for confronting with the transcendence and true love.

Great people recognize this subjective mirage because they have embraced true love and oneness.

140

True love is the understanding of the spiritual unity of each other, and the need for unlimited reconnection together.

And true unity is an interconnection to each other as independent members in the direction of the goals of the whole unit.

141

You always have enough reasons not to love someone because there is no perfect human being.

Unconditional love means loving someone who cannot love you and someone who cannot be loyal, honest, and selfless for you.

Ordinary people can only love a perfect human being that never exists and will not exist, but great people can accept and love you as you are incomplete.

142

You can truly love others when you have the inner ability to love someone who has closed her/his eyes to your heart.

143

A person who cannot love you and stay with you in pain and difficulty will never be able to love you unconditionally even in joy and welfare and cannot stay with you forever; and if he/she stays for some time, it will not be a reason for being in love with you.

144

Unconditional love is not just an expression of a feeling, but a reflection of the depths of your heart and soul.

The peace and beauty of your inner world manifest as unconditional love in the physical world.

145

Unconditional love means opening your heart and your hands to others who each one of them is a member of our global unity.

146

You are not the only one to be loved by your spouse, your beloved unconditionally, but you must be like a sun that he or she loves other people and creatures better in the sunshine of your love.

In other words, your beloved is a great, warm, and shining sun in your life that illuminates the lovely existence of others like the moon.

The pure heart and soul relation of two lovers can be an endless source of illumination, warming, and love for other human beings and creatures.

147

Unconditional love means opening our hearts, spreading our minds, and embracing each other's soul as independent parts of global oneness.

YOUR FREENESS, LOVELINESS, AND DIVINENESS

A true lover is the one who can love you at the peak of suffering and problems.

149

Those who cannot allow their hearts to be touched by their lover will never be able to perceive the true love, oneness, and happiness.

Such people may think that power, money, and selfishness can cover their deepest inner needs.

After many years, they will realize that all of them were just mirages; however, they will try to keep their power, money, and selfishness.

They want to deceive themselves and others because they cannot accept that they were wrong for a lifetime and let to lose even their childish delights.

Money and power are just tools in your hands, not goals, and they cannot be an alternative for your need to love, be loved, and feel inner happiness.

150

Except for a few, most people may not be able to express their unconditional love in inappropriate and violent conditions.

So, we should try to create the right conditions for most people to love each other naturally.

The human community does not need emotional geniuses to become the spiritual leaders of the majority of people, but they can only be responsible for helping others to create the right conditions and replace the new values based on unconditional love and oneness.

151

Those who can sacrifice their interests for universal and humanitarian values, not for the personal interests of others, will be able to love themselves and other human beings and creatures unconditionally.

152

Unconditional love is the art of great people with inner power who have deep and profound knowledge and understanding about the wrong values and all kinds of crimes and inappropriate acts, not the ignorant and naïve people who due to being weak and fearful pretend they love others.

153

There is nothing sacred in this world, except the unconditional love that is in the depths of your heart and soul.

In other words, whatever doesn't open your heart and soul to love others unconditionally cannot be a sacred thing.

154

We will be able to establish peace in the world, only when love and philanthropy for us are more important than our beliefs and political boundaries and financial benefits.

155

Unconditional love is constantly alive, based on the unique love melody that is always being played in the depth of our heart and soul.

In other words, unconditional love is a divine dance based on permanent and live inner music and a global universal song in the privacy of our oneness.

156

Two people can live together and love each other at the same time, based on unconditional love, and the art of living and loving. Otherwise, they must choose one of these, being lovers or a couple.

If not being lovers, then they may become couples who do not pay attention to the unconditional love, and the art of living and loving, and may like, but cannot love each other for a lifetime truly.

157

In ordinary marriages, couples usually do not try to love each other unconditionally because they think they own their husband/wife, and they always will have time to love her/him.

They easily ignore the moments of co-existence and its hidden moments of happiness.

A real marriage is living and the cooperation of two free and divine human beings, based on true love and unity, in a common path for the creation of transcendental and extraordinary goals, and the manifestation of happiness, with the appreciation of each moment of being together.

158

Permanent attention to the art of life and love for the creation of happiness in life represents true love, not expensive gifts.

159

Unconditional love is not just a feeling, but a manifestation of being in love with the oneness.

Only those who their inner freedom and beauty are higher and more potent than their rational beliefs, incorrect values, problems, and obstacles can love unconditionally.

Unconditional love means -- "I love you, even if you don't understand why and how, or you cannot love unconditionally, because there is no ego to feel I'm separate from you."

In simple terms, there is no border between you and me to think that I'm a separate being from you, and I love you as another being, but there are just two free and godlike human beings, which are parts of the oneness in divine love with each other.

160

Unilateral, unconditional love is enough to love other human beings and creatures; however, mutual unconditional love is necessary for two people to be able to live, love and be happy beside each other forever.

161

Unconditional love is not about what I tell you, but how it can be shown to you.

162

The sun is still shining behind the clouds when we cannot see anything except thunderstorms.

In the same way, the one who loves you unconditionally cannot stop loving you, even at the height of misunderstanding, because love is a part of her/his being.

163

The most important thing in your life is your time.

You devote most of your time to the things and people who are more important to you, and to whom you love them.

Whoever loves you and cares for you unconditionally, even in the worst circumstances, will always have enough time for you, even if it's only for one minute.

164

Couples/lovers, who love each other unconditionally, can talk freely about everything, accept criticism of each other, and always find solutions to their problems together.

165

Your true beloved is someone who is always in your heart, even if there are an infinite number of physical barriers between you and her/him.

166

True love is based on our spirit and unity, not momentary emotions dependent on thoughts and mental imagery.

167

Unconditional love is not just lovemaking, but it is sometimes like a bitter medicine or painful surgery.

Unconditional love is exploring the depths of the soul and the existence of oneself and others.

When we can love unconditionally, we can understand the strengths, weaknesses, ugliness, and beauty, and despite all of them, we understand the unity among ourselves.

168

The one who genuinely loves you will never hide weak points of you and herself/himself but will inform you about them in a completely private way and is always ready to help you become a better and more transcendent person.

169

A surgeon splits your body, but great men and women are those who do surgery on the heart and soul of themselves, others, and on fundamental social values.

Those who love unconditionally may sometimes appear to be very merciless people, like a surgeon, but they want nothing but health, happiness, growth, and transcendence for you.

170

"True love" based relationship means spiritual bond and oneness between two people at the height of respect for each other's freedom and independence.

171

Lovemaking and connection between two lovers are like food for their hearts and soul.

One can't say I'm too busy and don't have time to eat, bathe, or take care of my needs.

Likewise, a lover can't say I'm too busy and have no time to communicate and make love with my beloved.

172

You can love unconditionally all human beings and creatures. However, you only need to "live with" the one who loves your freedom, presence, and existence lifelong.

173

True lovers are like two wings, and with the power of love and harmony, they can open their arms toward great and transcendent goals and happiness.

174

True love is the manifestation of the dance of oneness based on the universal tune of the truth.

175

True love closes your eyes and ears to false values and false realities, and it opens to you an incredible vision of world truth.

Others, who cannot understand the oneness, only see your closed eyes and ears. They think your eyes and ears have never seen and heard the facts as they did.

True love manifests the meaning of life and happiness deep within you, and others can understand nothing, but only something that the limitations of their perception can let to be understood.

176

True love is like the sun, and the art of loving tells us what we need to do while life's sky is cloudy and stormy or even when a solar eclipse occurs temporarily.

177

True love means enjoying the glory of self-giving and deep commitment to our oneness.

178

Some people think humanitarians are too naïve.

True love is based on a deep understanding of anger and hatred, and anti-humanism. Therefore, such people can protect their beliefs against all kinds of false values and love others despite all the hatred they face.

Ignorant and naïve people can never absolutely love because, in the awkward moments of life, all their beliefs, values, and dreams will be severely weakened or destroyed.

179

Sometimes true love is like a painful burning fire in the depths of our being to burn our ego and false beliefs. It clears up our soul and strengthens our ability to understand the true values.

180

Emotionless sex is the highest level of pleasure for those who do not understand true love and the lowest level of satisfaction for those who understand it.

In other words, sex is like a lamp when your inner world is dark, but true love is like a sun that lights up your entire world thousands of times and makes your life much more meaningful and valuable.

Only love-based sex is the highest level of pleasure and a divine and sacred act.

181

True love is not like a lamp that is dependent on the behavior of others, but like the sun, whether you see it or close your eyes to justify a world without a sun.

Eventually, you will encounter the truth.

182

True love manifests from the state of being which you cannot stop loving because it is not just a sensation or emotion, but part of your being and nature.

And true beloved is someone whom his/her presence and existence can increase this manifestation to the highest possible extent.

183

It is very enjoyable to be together as two lovers, but it is never enough to experience true happiness.

True happiness will manifest when two human beings, who love each other, can clear their hearts and soul for each other and let their love shine as one in the form of two divine creatures whom they cannot give each other anything except everything. Their oneness cannot be anything but pure love and true happiness.

184

You can never love, unconditionally, if you aren't able to forgive unconditionally.

185

When two hearts can touch each other, without having anything to lose, something will be manifested which its name is "true love."

186

Do not choose anything if you have only one choice and that is hatred, but always choose love, if there is a choice between love and hate.

Maybe, sometimes, it is not easy to choose between love and hatred, but for you to choose, you need an open heart and a great soul.

187

Unconditional love is not just two words, but the way of life which comes from the true and sincere nature that lets us understand that we are one.

188

When true love manifests in your heart and soul, you will realize that those whom their existence is filled with hatred are not your real enemy, but they are those who need your unconditional love.

The real enemies are the people whom their love depends on a political and economic relationship. Their love's light is like a candle; limited and transient.

Such love can light up your inner world when it is dark.

Otherwise, there will be no need to exist such candles to light up your inner world with a false love when the sun of true love manifests.

189

Only when the sun hides at night can candles light up around you.

You can trust those who love you based on a political and financial relationship, only when true love has not yet manifested.

190

True love never can fail, because it is not based on physical separation or togetherness, but it always comes from the depths of your heart and soul unconditionally.

When there is no true love, you feel a failure because you cannot light up your inner world with candles.

It is essential to be able to manifest your sun of love in the depth of your heart and soul and share your love, without expecting any candle to light up your illuminated inner world.

191

Love and accept others unconditionally, even if they cannot do that.

However, only live with someone who can love and accept you unconditionally.

192

You will never be able to love someone truly unless your heart and soul can be free from the limited laws of political, economic, and belief systems and let your true nature shine.

193

Those who are humanitarians wonder how there are very narrow-minded people who can easily commit crimes and cruelties.

Those who do not care about love and humanity cannot understand and stop false thinking about how there can exist naïve and ignorant human beings who sacrifice themselves and their interests for others.

194

True love comes from the depths of your nature and the originality when you can love those who may do not be able to understand you or even don't appreciate your sacrifices.

195

True love means sacrifice, and there is no love if there is no sacrifice.

Sacrificing for what, you might ask? Should you hurt your body?

Love-based sacrificing means letting your heart and soul dissolve into the depths of your beloved's heart and soul.

196

There is great and pure love when there is neither my benefit nor your benefit, but everything reflects our unity and oneness.

There is no need to sacrifice anything for the ego of another one, only because you love her/him.

Scarification is the ultimate goal of true love, but toward the manifestation of oneness and unity of lovers' heart and soul, not for each other's ego.

197

The same acid that is corrosive and destructive to ordinary metals is the benchmark of gold, and the same suffering and discomfort that cuts off any relationship is the validator of true love.

198

Love is a perception of oneness and not limited to an attractive opposite-sex human being to interpret it based on a desire only for sex. Love is a desire for oneness or the belief in being one with someone, a creature, or something that we feel him/her/it as part of our being and our lives.

199

True love is our inner consciousness revolution for someone or something against our expired thoughts, beliefs, feelings, and values of the past.

The inner enlightenment is the reunification of our inner consciousness and the collective unconscious for the oneness against the limited awareness of being separated from the global consciousness.

200

Two lovers must respect each other's physical and mental privacy.

However, if there is any boundary between their heart and soul, and both or one of them would not break it, then it will be a sign that there is no pure and true love from someone who wants to keep the borders.

201

Being in love is not based on the feeling that I meet and want to be closer to someone else whom I love. This is only a pseudo-love, and there is no true and pure love.

Being in love is the perception that there is another part of my being that my heart and soul wants to embrace and unite with her/him, like organ transplants, but emotionally and spiritually.

202

The financial benefits are based on your separation from others.

True love is based on the perception of your unity with others who are part of your oneness.

They are like night and day and never come together.

When you have true love, you can never have a boundary between the monetary interests of yours and your beloved.

And if there is any boundary, then the love is not valid, but an emotional, political show under the name of love.

203

There is no feeling, thought, or power that can change anyone deep inside, except pure and true love.

True love is not just a simple and intense feeling.

So, what is the difference between an intense feeling and true love?

Sometimes an intense feeling manifests, which we think is love.

It is based on an explosion of our feelings and intense focus on someone/something. It has a starting point and an endpoint, and our view and belief system can raise it up or bring it down. This changes our emotional level which is variable.

True love manifests from our soul and raises us up and out of control of our belief system, thoughts, and feelings to see the divine beautifulness of the one whom we love. This changes our consciousness level which is fundamental and stable.

204

If someone opens her/his heart and body in the case of getting money from someone, this is not a relationship, but it has a negative name which you know better. Having a business with heart and body is a kind of immoral business and not a love-based relationship.

205

When a pseudo-love, intense emotional fascination, is in your heart, you may love one person strongly, and others are worthless for you or even you probably dislike them. Your view and feelings can change in a problematic situation, once the place of love and hatred reverses.

When true love manifests in your existence, the love between yourself and your beloved changes your view and perception, and it reveals the beautifulness and the value of others.

In other words, you will understand that others are divine creatures who can shine like bright stars, and your beloved is the closest star that shines like a sun on your soul and warms-up your heart.

This is the moment you fall in love with your beloved, and you love others unconditionally.

206

True love does not mean sacrificing yourself for the ego of someone else whom you love.

True love is not about fading "me" for "you."

If there is such an expectation, then this is only sacrificing true love for a fake love, and nothing more.

True love means being sacrificed in the depths of our hearts and souls to manifest oneness and unity beyond the perception of being "you" or "me."

True love is not like putting oxygen and hydrogen in the same place to let them remain unchanged, but their nature must lead to light and heat and explosion and manifest as water.

The light and heat and explosion need to come from the depths of our hearts and souls.

Your Divineness

207

So far, the best and most valuable thing we, as humans, have come to realize is love.

We have reached a level of awareness that we can understand the value of love.

Now, our understanding of the future is extremely limited.

If our understanding is deepened and expanded, then we can understand that love is the minimum of the necessary values in human society, life, and the world. We will realize that there can be values far beyond the love that we have so far failed to understand.

In the same way that a child who has not yet matured, for example, cannot understand the sexual relationship.

208

We perceive some new concepts above our thinking and feeling and as a reflection of the absolute truth. When our dominant emotions and thoughts grow to the extent of those new concepts, we will realize they are no longer responsive to us, but there must be much higher concepts and greater truth.

The process goes on forever, and surely any truth we reach into and transform our lives can lead to a higher understanding that transforms our lives even more in a way that we can grow to a new and higher truth based on our previous knowledge.

209

To know and to have much information is not enough for success and happiness.

We may know and learn many things, but we can only use our knowledge sufficiently for our happiness and success to the extent that our capacity for perception and understanding allows.

Whenever our mental and emotional capacity is too high or growing too fast, we can use our knowledge to the highest possible benefit for ourselves even if we don't have enough knowledge; we can get it quickly or find it with analytics and experience.

210

Life is only one path and no destination.

211

Although life can cover rewards or losing rewards, the purpose of life is not to get to a particular place or to obtain exclusive rewards.

The nature of life encompasses a perpetual path to perfection, with or without the existence of rewards.

212

If you want to go beyond the thoughts and feelings and words that you understand, immerse yourself in other people's thoughts, feelings, their inner language, culture, experiences and sciences, and always make this a part of your life to open your mind and heart to extend the power of your understanding.

213

The spiritual journey occurs in the very near past moments and in a situation where there is a need for excellence and perfection. The process is infinite and cannot lead to a particular point in the name of absolute perfection.

In the inner illumination and understanding of the present moment, it is the utmost perfection and divineness in which the journey is meaningless.

214

Some people say that if you laugh, you will likely be happy, or if you pretend to do good things, goodness manifests within you. Although they may have some effect on us for some reason, they are not effective.

These people often do things reluctantly and suffer from remaining far from their true identity and personality. Not only they do not have a fundamental change within but also a feeling increases that they are doing something especially important and honorable to their relatives and community, etc. , but not for themselves. That's why they must do it so painstakingly, painfully, and sacrificially. It seems they make sacrifices, and others become indebted to them.

When warming a piece of metal, it becomes hot, but it cannot turn into light. It can be brought to the level of radiant heat; however, it is still fleeting and with the disappearance of the external temperature, its true and more stable identity manifests.

The change must begin within with diverse experiences, knowledge, perceptions, happiness, goodness, and so on, albeit little but genuinely reinforced and manifested from within.

215

You may be wondering why I set such great goals that I may never reach them. They could be fulfilled, after hundreds of years.

Because the goals have a different meaning for me, I try to live for the present, and not the beliefs of the past!

Our emotions and minds must be so big and open that we deserve that purpose.

If our minds and emotions are perfectly consistent with the goals, then great goals manifest, such as what happened to Gandhi, Martin Luther King, and thousands of other great people.

I want to live in and for a world based on global love culture and try to make my inner life look like that and manifest it.

Maybe in my lifetime, I can't reach any goal; it doesn't matter because the true meaning of life is on the path to my goals, and the joy, happiness, and excitement of this exciting journey to create a better and more beautiful world is enough for me.

To create a global love culture in the physical world, billions of other people like me, and you have to make that decision.

If our human minds and hearts accept unconditional love, at this very moment, the global love culture manifests and does not need hundreds of years. Isn't it possible to have this thought and feeling?

Of course, if I say I want to travel out of the Milky Way and live on another planet, now that isn't realistic because there is no such possibility for anyone in the world because the technology doesn't exist. That doesn't mean it won't happen in the future.

However, if there is something possible in the world, it can be evidence that there is a high probability that similar things can widely be created and developed.

If one person can love humanity unconditionally, others will be able, too, and the global love culture will be created like a spark that can turn into light and heat in the right conditions.

Either way, no matter what to get or not.

The value of our lives is based on the quality of our minds and real feelings.

When your pure thoughts and feelings are in a particular direction, you move in the same direction.

When you dance, you dance. Life is like a dance. You can dance (live) better only with a stronger thought and feeling.

104

Live for life as the best you and forget about reaching a specific destination in the future.

The best kind of life we can have is to live by nature, our talents, our interests, our needs, and our abilities as we grow and excel in this direction.

A flower does not care if it will die shortly, but it is only alive and manifests its true nature, and the existence and life have the same meaning for other creatures.

Goal setting is crucial because it determines our path of life and movement, but in any case, life is a process, not a destination.

216

Others around us are part of our oneness. We see the inadequacy of our unity when confronted with adverse situations and behaviors from others.

When we perceive beauty, pleasant behaviors, and conditions, we witness the perfection and the positive points of our oneness.

217

My words are not absolute truth but are perspectives toward a truth that you can only understand within yourself. These words can be complemented by your and others' intuitive understandings, like a puzzle to manifest an image of the truth.

218

The truth of one person's life and success can be different from another.

I or others can share our knowledge and experiences with you, but our way of success is different.

By imitating the lifestyle of others, you destroy your authentic life and identity.

The path to success is in the way of your true talents and interests.

You can be a great man or woman.

If you want to become a great human being, keep in touch with and learn as much as you can from the great humans of the world, but if you become a captive and an imitator, you have lost your way.

If you notice people around, you can see those great people never imitate others.

Those who say that our way, our thoughts, our belief, our speech, and our behavior are the truth, are the greatest enemies of humankind that impede the love and unity of humanity.

Remember, genuinely great people are those who strive to help others to become great themselves.

219

The power of great men and women rests on their inner strength, not on the position and condition of external forces.

If you want to find your way and become a great person, consider the following:

- Know the values of your personal life.

- Discover your talents, interests, and abilities.

- Identify your strengths and weaknesses.

- Set your own goals.

What are the secret of great humans and world masterpieces?

First, study, practice, and learn as much as possible. Also, meditate on what you have learned and analyze it.

If you live and teach others based on your knowledge, you will be a regular teacher and master, but if you do not use your expertise, you can become a great person!

Always learn, but let go of your knowledge and wait, because your real understanding and real awareness are born! Your existence must be like a river of wisdom, not an archive of knowledge.

Sometimes, exciting, positive, meaningful ideas and content suddenly come to your mind. Always write down those ideas. These are inspirations of your inner guide.

If you pay attention to these ideas and always write them down, they will flow, and more ideas will come to your mind.

That's the secret of great writers and speakers. Their formal content and remarks are not based on their ordinary and commonplace knowledge and ideas; instead, they try to fine-tune their ideas, which may even have been written over several years, then maybe present them as lectures or books. Their work comes from the depths of their existence and affects others profoundly. The effect can be immediate or occur long after publishing their ideas.

If you want to become a great person, apply these ideas to your daily life.

As the flow of these inner inspirations intensifies, you will gradually reach a stage where much of your thoughts and feelings will be based on this inner guidance.

At this point, you and your point of view will change, your services are love-based and unconditional, and no one in the world can replace you.

It doesn't matter if others can understand you, because in the end, only you are accountable to yourself, not to others. It is essential that your mind and emotions are in tune with the depth of your being and that you can move along the path of progress and transcendence.

Notice in your path that this is infinite. You can be a great person when you always move along this path of better and better. Greatness is a part of your core habits and characteristics.

If you want to unconditionally love, and serve yourself and humanity, no matter what your circumstances are, manifest your inner greatness and be a great human being.

Normally, our inner world is like a cluttered puzzle of a treasure map, and we can't see the whole image of the truth of the world to make big decisions in life.

If we look at our profound inner ideas and inspirations, the puzzle will repeatedly be rearranged, and finally, we will clearly see in it the beautiful image of our greatness and wealth. When this transpires, our lives change.

Lastly, I emphasize that you need to learn unlimited knowledge from others, but to become a great human being, do not imitate others' speech and behavior. Instead, focus on your deep ideas.

Great people do not need to be approved by ignorant and weak people who have no will.

Only fake masters and leaders can boast of ignorant, weak, and fanatical fans because they know that such people do not know the difference between true great men and false great men, that's why they exploit their ignorance.

Great people appreciate the approval of other great people and prefer to live among other great people as friends.

You may be one of the great people now or in the future.

220

Most people want to be great. These people do not know what the great people's secret is, so they try as much as they can to gain wealth, power, knowledge, and a position to prove to others that "they are great people and you are lesser and less valuable human beings."

Such people may have a great deal of knowledge and talent and have endured a great deal of suffering and hardship, but they have lost their way. However, they imagine that they are moving in the right direction.

If we jump from 1000 meters onto a rock, it doesn't matter if we are good people or not; we likely will die -- the laws of physics, especially the law of gravity, plays a role in the outcome.

Becoming a great human being and creating lasting works, like anything else in the world, has its own rules, and there is nothing by chance.

221

We assume you must go one hundred and one steps to become a great man or woman. After the one-hundredth step, you realize that your distance to become a great person seems to be only one step.

Many people pass the first hundred steps after years, but fewer can reach one hundred and one. Why? Because people make an incorrect calculation.

As you master a hundred steps, you realize that to pass the one hundredth and one step, you must sacrifice all your knowledge and experience gained in the previous one hundred steps, and also, you must try thousands of times more to pass beyond the hundredth step.

At the hundredth step, you think you are a great man or woman. You think the results of your one hundred-steps effort are precious. You think you don't need more to make more effort to transform.

If you think that way, you can never become a great man or woman.

If you've read the books written by great people a few years ago, reread them because it is a necessity to do so. A few years ago, you may not have understood some of their concepts and messages, and now that your mental capacity has increased, you can understand more and much more in-depth.

The world's masterpiece books are like an ocean of wisdom. When your mental capacity is as much as a cup, you can get enough of it even if your mind is as big as a lake; you can still get enough of it.

To create a global masterpiece, your mind and heart must be as vast as the ocean. The greatest feat of great men or women is not their works, but their personality.

Some people imagine a human being becoming a great person because they created a global masterpiece. No, it's the opposite!

A great man or woman builds his/her personality with the manifestation of his/her inner greatness, then his/her works become unconsciously global masterpieces.

Along the way, you imagine you are creating world masterpieces, but you are manifesting the great man or woman who you indeed are.

223

Even the greatest of humans can understand only part of the truth within themselves. These understandings are just a few pieces of the billions of the global puzzle pieces that give us an overall image of the truth and unity of the world.

There is no great man or woman who can understand the whole truth. Likewise, no one can convey her/his pure inner understanding of the truth to others. Why? A direct understanding of the truth is completely personal.

But when great people come together, they can understand each other's inner experiences with true love, and develop their view of the truth of the world.

Great people by words cannot transfer their personal understanding of the truth to others, and once they try to do that, it generates disagreement and division among the people who mistakenly believe the truth.

Great people can only understand themselves by themselves, and although their presence and existence are inspirational to others, they cannot be great instead of others.

Copying and counterfeiting of the greatness of other humans are useless.

You can't become a great person by copying global masterpieces.

You have no choice but to be a great human by being yourself.

224

In the path of knowledge, you will reach a stage where you think you know many things. Then you come to a stage where you realize that not only you do not know much, but even what you do know may be wrong.

Thereupon, your heart and mind will be opened.

The time to understand... from then on...

Our family will be humanity-sized, and the world and our home will be exactly alike -- an excessively big home in people's hearts and a world without borders.

This is the first step in the path of manifestation of inner wisdom, greatness, and unconditional love.

Now let yourself feel the most beautiful feeling in the world -- to feel your unity with oneness and happiness.

225

A professional man strives to show the greatness and beauty of nature and others in his works in the best feasible way, but a great man manifests his/her inner truth and greatness in her/his works.

226

Those who try to speak the details of their inner truth to anyone and impose it on others, violate and mislead others, but assume they are doing the right thing.

This is like a lecturer who speaks to people and thinks if children heard his/her lecture about sexual issues they must be able to understand the pleasure of sex, and when the children do not understand what he/she is talking about, thinks the children are stupid!

This is wrong. If children can't understand this; are children stupid or are we violating their childhood identity? As a child grows up freely and naturally, he or she can understand this without the need for others.

Such work is like the false enlightenment of an ignorant person by a drug. While enlightenment comes naturally after the growth and excellence of consciousness, it is genuine and valuable.

If you let people grow naturally and you are an inspiration to them, ignorance and prejudice will be the only temporary stages in the slowly changing lives of individuals, and they will begin to understand love and humanity and valid values.

Just as a five-year-old child does not suddenly become a forty-year-old, usually, there is no shortcut to becoming a great man or woman.

227

As a human being, you have two different choices:

First choice: You can believe that you are the best or the most powerful or the wisest person in the world.

In such situations, you will focus more on people's weaknesses and ignorance.

Your mind and feelings will be filled with a lot of weakness, ignorance, and imperfections you see around the world.

Then, you either deem most people completely worthless and hate to contact with others as much as possible, or you base your life subconsciously on ignorance and inadequacies to coordinate and work in the society.

You know your path is wrong, but you persuade yourself over the years that you can make your life full of love and happiness.

At this point, you have signed your failure certificate.

Eventually, you realize that you have lost your life, and after a lifetime of trying to find the happiness you found something that is only a mirage, but you have to be bigoted and pretend to be happy in front of others, or commit suicide or commit a crime.

Second choice: You believe in the oneness of the world and strive to manifest the unity of the world better, more powerful, and wisely.

You see more and better the uniqueness, the greatness, and the beauty of the creatures, and human beings.

Your mind and feelings are full of beauty and glory.

You consciously base your life on the foundation of oneness, love, beauty, and greatness.

You and others enjoy each other's existence and presence.

Many people may open their hearts and souls to you.

Their oneness, greatness, and beauty are manifested in you.

At this point, the world has allowed you to succeed and excel.

You will be immortalized without any effort, and your behavior, thought, and feelings will transcend the heart of humanity throughout history.

Hitler and Martin Luther King were both raised in difficult conditions and were both geniuses.

The most important thing that caused the sharp contrast in their lives was two different viewpoints.

Hitler, according to his illusory perspective, used his ingenuity in the path of racism, anti-humanism, and crime; whereas Martin Luther King, with his exalted view, used his ingenuity in the path of oneness and humanity and love.

Your condition may be inappropriate and even your body in chains, but in the end, you can choose your point of view and change your thinking, feelings, beliefs, and lives, and finally transform the world.

Some people may say that our main problem is that we do not know how to change our perspective.

If you don't know how to swim, swimming is hard and tough for you, and if you can swim well, swimming is a dance in the water.

The difference between failure and success lies in this point.

Do you want your viewpoint to be uplifted?

The secret is amazingly simple.

If you let yourself be a truth seeker, with the pure ideas of your inner guide, you learn to swim in the ocean of your interests, talents, and abilities, and succeed with joy, pleasure, and without a special effort, transform your vision, and eventually become a great person.

228

Some people think that by bigotry and closing their minds and hearts, they are protecting their security.

They think they have valuable knowledge, beliefs, thoughts, and feelings that they should take care of like a treasure.

These people do not realize that this will corrupt both their mental and emotional assets and impede their understanding of the secrets of their success and excellence.

Money and property are limited, and, naturally, you cannot give them to anyone, but your inner wealth is endless. Open your inner treasury to the world wholeheartedly and unconditionally.

After a while, your inner love and wealth will become so intense that it will be astonishing to yourself and others.

Over the short-term or long-term, depending on social and environmental conditions, you will notice that the shadow of the barriers and constraints of the world will fade away in the light of your love and generosity.

229

Some people identify themselves as spiritual people. They say they have come to inner illumination.

But how can you recognize them?

If they have such experiences, they can understand the oneness of the world, and in such conditions, they genuinely and unconditionally love other human beings and creatures and are even willing to sacrifice some of their interests for the sake of others.

If these people aren't sure their experiences are illusory, they rise for some time in deep, tangible illusions like a drug addict.

These experiences are sometimes even more tangible than physical facts for them.

On the one hand, one seeks for more and greater pleasures for oneself, and on the other hand, (s)he thinks that (s)he is a great man or woman and even is a God and others must obey her/him as a slave.

Such people have fallen into the valley of ignorance on the path of excellence. These people can't help you.

They are like very thirsty people lost in the desert. They think they see the sea, but what they see is nothing but a permanent mirage.

Great people have no fundamental difference with other human beings; their only significant difference with other human beings is that they have discovered the secret to love and serve better to themselves, others, and the world.

In short, great people can love those who are not loved by many people and can serve in a friendly manner to people who are unworthy of others.

I do not agree with all of Gandhi's and Mother Teresa's views, but both were examples of a great man and woman. At the same time, you can see many fake great people in the world.

230

On the path to transcendence, you must be free from all your prior knowledge and beliefs. It should be noted that this does not mean that your knowledge and beliefs are worthless and that you must fight them, not that it is not true.

The truth is when you were younger and more unaware, you needed them, and you don't need them in the higher stages of your personality transcendence.

In the process of greater awareness and transcendence, you feel this needlessness within yourself.

Release yourself from that bondage.

This is very simple. You never say that the clothing I wore as a child was sacred and that I have to wear it for the rest of my life.

231

Let's suppose I have a genuinely nice, good, and expensive dress that I have worn since childhood. With other fabrics, I stretch it a little every year to make it fit my size. I inherited this dress from my ancestors, and they told me it is very sacred.

This dress is even more sacred than my body and soul. Without this dress, I would have no value. The previous generation who gave me this dress told me that it protects me from the cold, even in the middle of Antarctica.

I want to wear it for the rest of my life and also want it to be my shroud. I have a lot of these same clothes. Anyone approaching me will forcibly wear this dress.

Believe me; if you wear this outfit, you can be happy forever and get a jewel-filled palace.

Am I stupid living this way? Yes, you are right.

Dears, what I mentioned above was a metaphor. Now I have forgotten this dress.

This dress is nothing but your past dead knowledge and beliefs about the truth.

Do not hold or burn this dress. Leave it to those in need and find and wear an article of new and fit clothing. In other words, don't stop at this point and know that there are always higher steps.

Re-read the above and look in the mirror and repeat the above question and realize that the truth is what is alive and fresh in the depths of our hearts, souls, and oneness.

Always revolutionize your mind and feelings and beliefs so that a living truth is the basis of your life.

Are you looking for life in the cemetery? Of course not. The books written about the truth are the lifeless body of the truth.

If you want to be a historian of truths, read the books which are about the truth in all your life, but if you want to become a great human being, leave the graveyard of the truth. The true and living truth is at the depth of your own heart and existence.

Not even my words are alive anymore. They contained a message and are now dead.

Leave it for those in need. Be free from my words and let yourself perceive the truth directly and deep inside yourself.

232

As a child, you are innocent, lovely, and ignorant of the oneness of the world, and your original identity is visible.

When unconditional love becomes part of your existence, as you perceive the oneness of the world, your childhood charm is reborn within you, you re-experience the beautiful feelings of childhood, and your genuine and authentic identity is re-manifested.

At this point, you are communicating with your original identity, and this is the first step in the path of incredible changes in the life and creation of global masterpieces.

233

In the course of researching, analyzing, and meditating on the facts of the universe, you become a very thoughtful, earnest, and emotionless person.

Once you understand the oneness of the universe, love and happiness will gradually erupt in your existence, and your treatment to other people will be friendly and intimate.

At this point, know that you are on the right track for real growth and excellence.

234

If you can understand the oneness of the world, you go beyond your ego and express love unconditionally; your personality will not crush with any lies, insults, or humiliations by others. In such a situation, your existence rests on the greatness within you, not the unstable external forces.

235

In the early stages of our inner journey, we imagine we are on the path to the truth and oneness, but that may not be the case.

Because if the truth is in the inner world, there must not be so many different and contradictory ideas that take us away from oneness.

All the different ideas and beliefs have come from the depths of our inner worlds. These have many common points and points of difference.

The outside and the inner worlds are two parts of oneness.

In our minds, we imagine the oneness of the world as two separate inner and outer worlds.

Any change in the outside world can affect our inner world, and so any change in our inner world can affect the physical world.

Both the inner and outer worlds are parts of the realities of our existence and our lives. I emphasize that none of these are the truth but only the reality of our lives.

When you can perceive the real existence and true present moment, we understand something beyond the inner and outer worlds, and that is the unity of the whole outward and inward existence.

There are times and entities in both worlds but in diverse ways. The inner world may be fascinating and infinite, but it is, in any case, dependent on physical factors. For example, you cannot go into the depths of your inner world under any circumstances.

When time and entity become meaningless, or in other words, we understand the true existence and true present moment at a zero point, then we can understand the truth of oneness.

At this point, both the inner and outer worlds are meaningless. Understanding the oneness goes beyond this.

236

Imagine a prominent climber climbing Mount Everest!

Such a person was undoubtedly a child many years ago who couldn't even climb a stairwell.

If you want to become a great person, consider yourself a child on the path to progress and excellence, and imagine all your current knowledge and achievements as a child's toy.

Live physically or virtually among the world's great humans.

Open your mind and heart unconditionally and allow yourself to grow naturally.

Over the years, your mind and feelings will grow older and stronger.

Some thoughts and forces manifested in you that are hundreds of times more powerful.

In such a situation, you will realize that if you have been struggling for years to understand something, now you can understand it in less than a minute.

Why? Because you used to think you were separate from the world, and your connection to the oneness was cut off, and your ability was limited, but now your connection to the oneness is established, and your ability is vast.

You can easily understand the oneness of humanity and the world.

How do you feel when you realize you are part of the greatness of the world and the greatness of the world is part of your existence?

Quite simply, you enjoy the presence of yourself and others as much as possible and love yourself and others unconditionally.

237

All our lives, we think we live for ourselves, but eventually, we realize that we have made a big mistake.

We are here to manifest the oneness, nothing else.

Whatever knowledge and experience we gain will eventually come buried with us, and we will lose everything else.

124

We can indeed have a valuable life when, based on our talents, interests, abilities, and understanding of the true present moment, we allow the oneness manifests, and we love unconditionally.

238

I have been researching since 1996 about different religions, mysticism, psychology, metaphysics, and so on.

Am I superior to others? If I think that to be true, I have gone astray.

All of them are worthless unless I understand their central message.

I'm not an emotionless computer and neither storing a library in my brain. That's not honorable.

Studying and researching is only a means of understanding and living a better life.

When we misplaced the device with the goal, and gaining more knowledge and experience becomes the primary purpose of our lives, we become further apart.

In such a situation, you can be a supercomputer, and eventually, all your software-like knowledge and experience will be buried with you.

If you're a wiser human being, you should be able to treat others with friendliness, understand the oneness of the universe, and unconditionally love others.

In such situations, you will be part of the heart and soul of the eternal oneness of the universe.

Let's suppose I fully understand this and want to be such a human being. Am I a good person, a saint, and should others respect me more? If I think to believe this concept, I am gravely mistaken!

Like other human beings, even a good and saintly person can be perverted.

I'm a scientist, a philanthropist, a saint, a great lover, and so on! This kind of thinking is low-minded. They are all worthless unless I try to help others to be more prominent scientists, saints, and lovers.

Ignorance and wisdom, impurity, and sacredness, ugliness and beauty, and good and bad are relative things intertwined in different situations and are, in fact, different faces of each other. Oneness is something more than those, and out of imagination and beyond description.

We are all parts of the oneness. Our goodness and beauty are part of the oneness of others, and the ugliness and badness of others are parts of our oneness.

239

Can't you unconditionally love yourself? If you said yes, you are right!

The true existence of all of us is the oneness. Under normal circumstances, we have simulated oneness as our ego.

Our ego sees itself as everything, but it's just a ghost in the darkness that becomes meaningless by the light of the oneness.

When this ego spell leaves our being, we see that the distance between you and me is meaningless. I can absolutely love you, and in fact, I love my true self that is in the depths of your heart and soul.

240

We always have different personalities within us.

If we are healthy, these different personalities are interconnected and harmonious, but if the connections of different personalities within us are interrupted, we will suffer from various mental illnesses.

A multi-character human being is inconsistent with himself or herself and sometimes does the opposite of what he or she did a few hours ago and may not be able to believe that maybe has from two to hundreds different personalities, and other personalities who have previously done different things are all parts of him or her.

It is not about discussing distinct roles and states in different circumstances and based on a single identity. Instead, it is meant to be about people who are not personality stable and have several different, even antagonistic, and heterogeneous core identities.

We usually, as humanity's society, are a oneness of countless personalities like a multi-personality human being, and we have lost contact with other characters of our oneness.

When we are interconnected with our other oneness characters and can accept their harmony, we find that if someone in the corner of the world is a good man and also if there is a criminal on the other side of the world, both are different faces of our oneness.

In such a situation, while we confirm goodness and reject crime, we can accept conflicting characters as part of our oneness.

The good and the bad, and the ugliness and the beauty of me and you, and others are all parts of the coordinated or uncoordinated characteristics of our oneness.

By understanding our oneness, we can perceive a truth beyond good and evil and opposing poles.

This is a mystery that all great men like Martin Luther King and Gandhi have come to realize.

Each of us, as a cell, is part of the oneness, and the brain of that oneness is the wisdom and guidance within us.

If you find that I am part of you and others, and you are part of me and others, how do you think, feel, and behave?

It's so simple, with a great sense of responsibility and a strong relationship with the universe and the creatures, paradise will appear in your inner world in an incredible and wonderful way!

Your existence and the oneness will have an equal value to you. You will be able to love unconditionally, and therefore, as a great human being and part of the honors of human society, you will be immortalized.

241

After years of researching different religions, mysticism, psychology, metaphysics, etc., I have come to know many great people.

Based on my own experiences, I endorse one person more than anyone else.

I would recommend Osho's films and books to those who are in the preliminary stages of self-development and transcendence.

I am not following Osho or anyone else, but after years of experience and inner journeys, I have come to remarkably similar perceptions and conclusions and confirm that Osho's words originate from a source of pure truth.

Remember, try to eventually become a great man or woman yourself and get rid of the thoughts and feelings and beliefs of others, even other great people.

Nobody can become a great man or woman by copying and following others.

The great men and women were great because they manifested their uniqueness.

242

Always follow the humanitarian and right ideas, not good people!

The good and the bad in the world are relative and variable.

A positive man or woman cannot always be positive, and a negative person is not always negative.

If, in the future, my behavior and speech were inhumane and inaccurate, follow your inner wisdom.

If some of my content is not clear to you, please know that you do not need them now, and you can reread the book in the next years.

In any case, follow your heart.

There is no perfect human.

Why are the teachings of some great men or women inconsistent? Because even the capacity of enlightened people is limited, and they can understand only part of the truth.

Sometimes, the intuition is based on the unconscious mind and not the truth.

I or others may unconsciously distract you because of ignorance.

Your inner guide knows your needs and guides you on the path to progress and excellence.

Try to understand your inner guide and depend solely on your inner wisdom. It is something beyond your ordinary thoughts and feelings and beliefs.

243

If you can understand the oneness, you realize that the boundary between the inner world and the physical world is unreal. Both are closely related parts of our existence.

If most people are weak within, they can have a negligible impact on others and the physical world. They lose contact with their inner world if they suffer severe problems in the physical world.

If I say that you rely on your inner guidance, it does not mean that our world is entirely independent of the physical world.

Instead, it is the inner world where we can better understand our talents, interests, abilities, and genuine existence.

The physical world is infinite and may contain inaccurate social rules and many imperfections. In the same way, our inner world is infinite and may be created based on our own and others' defective thoughts, feelings, needs, beliefs, and environmental conditions.

Overall, the inner world is more rooted, more confident, more powerful, and more honest about recognizing ourselves and moving on the path of progress and excellence.

The inner world is the manifestation place of our inner wisdom and not the truth.

Like a physical force and analysis based on our physical abilities, we have the power of enlightenment and extraordinary actions based on inner wisdom, and they have nothing to do with the truth.

The truth is neither based on any part of the world, the outside, nor the inner world.

Discovery and intuition are not enough in our inner world, but we must be able to communicate and coordinate between our inner and physical worlds and to others and other creatures.

131

In such situations, we understand something beyond the inner and outer worlds, good and bad, space and time, and being -- that is the oneness.

Great wise words are based on inner guidance and wisdom, and not the truth.

Ordinary experiences and knowledge are the indirect and opaque effects of the truth, and the inner wisdom is the more direct and transparent effect of the truth.

However, the truth itself is indescribable.

Personal truth can only be understood directly and in the true present moment -- the moment when the oneness of humanity and the world manifests in you and unconditional love becomes part of your natural attributes.

This global understanding and puzzle must also be perfected by all of us so that we can understand the universal truth of oneness, or be born, in other words, as the truth and oneness.

You must become familiar with your inner wisdom and that of others and break their boundaries permanently to manifest the oneness and the truth in your existence.

That's why I say my words are based on my inner perceptions and not the truth.

Your knowledge and experience or your inner wisdom should be a means of progress and excellence and understanding of the truth and oneness. If you depend on knowledge and experience and inner wisdom alone, you will not be able to understand the truth. You need to go beyond them.

Your inner knowledge and experiences are like water that purifies the container of your existence from ignorance so that the truth and oneness can manifest in you.

If you want to experience the truth and oneness, get rid of your caged thoughts, feelings, and beliefs.

244

Powerful people strive to expand your heart and mind so they can be part of the popular people in your inner world, but weak people restrict your heart and mind, by force and threat, to make you part of the objects of their physical world.

245

The stages of understanding the truth, the true present moment, and the oneness are as follows:

- Discover and live by your talents, interests, and abilities.
- Be a scientist in the physical world.
- Be wise in the inner world.
- Always break the boundaries of physical knowledge and inner wisdom.
- Finally, you realize that all your knowledge and wisdom have been useless, and you are deeply frustrated.
- At the height of frustration, you are freed from the shackles of your knowledge, wisdom, and existence.
- Suddenly, beyond the inner and outer worlds, the truth and oneness manifest in your being.

246

Do you think you have to be a philosopher or follow a particular group or beliefs to understand the truth? This concept is a misconception.

Every human is unique.

Philosophers, for example, want to discover the truth in the path of their talent and interest, that is, philosophy.

You can also walk the path of the truth if you move on your talents, interests, and abilities.

If you are not a philosopher, you do not need the truth of what philosophers say.

247

If you can understand the oneness, look at anyone and everything, ugly or beautiful, you will find yourself in it as if looking in the mirror.

At this moment, you are indeed the manifestation of the greatness of the world, and the world will see its greatness in you.

Suddenly you realize that you are in global lovemaking. This is how the inner world of a great man or woman is.

248

Knowledge is like light, and the inner wisdom is like night vision.

249

If you progress only based on the physical world without regard to the inner world, you will be like a tree in the desert. Eventually, you will die of thirst.

If you move in the path of transcendence only based on the inner world, regardless of the physical world, you will be like a tree on the surface of the sea. You will be overwhelmed by a wave.

Some people want you to be without the blessings of the physical world and take your wealth from you. They want you to be a weak spiritual person and to control you to cover their lack of love and affection through your attention and respect.

Other people keep you away from love and spirituality to take you away from the treasure and joy of the inner world.

They want you to be a non-spiritual and ignorant human being to impose their beliefs on you as spiritual leaders and saints and to compensate by you their lack of finances.

Strive to spread your roots in the inner world and to excel as much as possible in the physical world.

Unconditional love means to love all aspects of your life. You must love both your soul and your body.

You're like a rope walker who must get across the rope.

If you lose your balance and are inclined to one of the sides, physical or inner world, you fall, anyway.

If only the physical world or only the inner world is your goal, you will go astray on an infinite path.

Try to use both to reach beyond them, namely love and oneness.

If you have no choice and cannot coordinate between the physical and the inner world, choose the inner world. Because you'd better be a paralyzed alive human being, not an animated soulless dead.

250

At the beginning of your life, you are like a chicken in an egg.

Your thoughts and feelings and beliefs are like eggshells that guarantee your safety.

You learn to tighten the shell to protect yourself.

Hold on! This is completely wrong!

On the path to progress and excellence, you no longer need past thoughts, feelings, and beliefs.

Break this shell; otherwise, until the end of your life, you must accept a small, cramped, lifeless world as absolute truth, and you will be buried alive in your little world.

If you break this shell and let go of the thoughts, feelings, and beliefs of yours, mine, and others', you can be born into an immensely tremendous and wonderful world.

If the physical world of someone separates from others, and the universe resembles an egg and its inner world is as large as the earth, the world of someone who can understand the oneness is as vast as the entire universe. Please note that I mean a world beyond the outer and inner worlds, which are the world of oneness.

251

You think you understand the truth, but you are in deep collective hypnosis.

Many of the values in your life are all simulated in your mind, and they are not true.

In this situation, your brain waves are at the Beta level, and you are overwhelmed by social thoughts and emotions.

To be able to reprogram your subconscious, you need to control the Alpha wave of your brain.

In such situations, you can fully control your mind and feelings, regardless of the negative or positive environmental conditions.

The stronger brain waves of phenomenally successful people are Alpha, not Beta.

Unsuccessful people are often in deep social hypnosis, and their brain waves are at Beta level.

Extraordinarily successful people are often subconsciously deep in a kind of self-hypnosis, and their brain waves are at the Alpha and Theta levels.

252

Under normal circumstances, you live according to the outward symbols of the world and the different masks of others.

Great humans can see the concepts and relevance of the symbols of the world and the true existence of humans and creatures and their relationship and live as part of the oneness.

253

All the different shapes of the world and the various masks of yourself and others are interconnected.

The meaning of different things is not in their differences.

First, you read these words. Second, you get rid of these words. Then, you try to understand the unit concept that lies in these words.

Every different being is like a word from the book of the truth of the universe, and the oneness is the concept of the content of this book.

254

If you no longer exist in this world, will your empty place feel in the world?

In other words, do you feel that a robot or another person can replace you in the world?

If that is the case, I suggest that you change the course of your life.

Under these circumstances, your life is a copy, not an original.

255

If you cannot rule over your talents, interests, and abilities, you will have to obey others according to their talents, interests, and abilities.

256

The present moment and your true existence have no beginning and no end. Whatever you have achieved in the past will inevitably be lost in the future.

Living based on the past and the future equals a sense of false wealth and pleasure, and then a severe inner vacuum evolves.

This false circle is repeated infinitely, and in the end, you get to the absurdity of life.

257

Usually, we have lost our connection with the greatness and unity of the world.

We are in a constant spiritual vacuum and unconsciously simulate the oneness of the world in our inner world.

This world looks very real, but in essence, it's nothing but a mental mirage.

We imagine that if we become more knowledgeable, wealthy, and more capable, which does not match our true talents and interests, our inner vacuum will fade away, but it does not.

258

The fetuses in the womb of their mothers and the dead in their graves are entirely independent and alone!

There are infinite creatures in this world that you can communicate with and not be alone. If you negatively feel you are alone in the world, your true being is not yet born or dead!

In such situations, you have lost your connection to life, the world, and other creatures.

In such situations, you must simulate your life, the world, and your relationships.

If you can understand your connection to other beings, you will feel alone again and embrace positivity, but this being alone is based on an understanding of the greatness and uniqueness of the world in your being that eliminates the inner need for the constant presence of others, because you understand that everyone is part of your being and that there is a perpetual subtle connection.

You will genuinely connect with life, other beings, and the world, and these authentic relationships are based on the unconditional love that connects our hearts and souls.

259

Do you know what the secret of the men and women who pretend to be great but are not, is?

Quite simply, they try to make others believe in unreal things that are beyond comprehension and undeniable.

Logic cannot resist an undeniable illusion.

They indirectly put you in a hypnotic state and take control of your subconscious mind.

These people seem to speak of human unity, but in practice, they are the cause of the spread of separation and division among people.

The appearance, speech, and behavior of forgers of greatness are remarkably similar.

Do you know how to get to recognize a great man or woman?

Quite simply, based on her/his belief in the oneness of all beings and the universe, can sacrifice many of his/her interests to those who have no benefit for her/him. And s/he can unconditionally love those who are his/her enemy and will never understand her/him.

The laws of the world are very different from the economic laws of human society.

The laws of giving and receiving in the world are unconditional.

The law of cause and effect is not based on good and bad, but on unconditional universal principles.

Good and bad are human characteristics, not universal principles.

Global unity and unconditional love are beyond goodness and badness.

To transform our lives, we must rethink our values based on universal law.

Good and bad are part of the ego. When your ego disappears and oneness manifests, goodness and badness become meaningless, and you unconditionally love good and bad, ignorant and scientist, rich and poor, wise and foolish people.

Gandhi was an example of liberated people from the belief in good and bad Karma.

In general, it doesn't matter if you're a good or bad person, and it doesn't even matter if you're a human. In any case, when it rains, it rains unconditionally.

Any creature can use oxygen as much as it wants; the sunlight is unconditional, and so on.

That's real-world rules. Our world is based on unlimited and unconditional givenness for all the creatures.

All creatures in the world manifest themselves based on their innate talents and abilities. For example, when the sun shines and publishes light and heat, this is part of its potential. Here the goodness and expectation of rewards are entirely pointless.

Good, for an inherently good human being, is like breathing and flushing out carbon dioxide. If your goodness is based on your essence, abilities, and interests, you will not need rewards.

An example of such a man was Martin Luther King, who said we need to love our enemies too. Such a person cannot accept the Karma based on badness and goodness and believe that some people deserve to be tormented.

If you are not a good person by nature, but by economic rules you are trying to be good so that others will reward you, you are lost. True goodness is an intrinsic quality and not a financial transaction.

Under such circumstances, you can never understand oneness and unconditional love.

Many of our problems are merely the product of our limited thoughts, feelings, and beliefs.

We have transformed the lives of many into a great tragedy by limiting the boundary between humans and rationing unlimited resources.

The climax of unconditional love is to return to your original talents and abilities and the manifestation of the essence of your existence.

Unconditional love means believing in a world that is unconditional for me, and for such a world, I unconditionally live based on the true nature of my existence.

261

If you want to move on the path of excellence, never wait for others to criticize you.

Open your mind and heart and be your most prominent critic in self-diagnosis toward improvement.

Some people may not accept the facts, but you can rest assured they can recognize the truths within.

Also, an expert can quickly identify facts based on the disharmony of the body's natural actions, speech, and reactions.

If you neglect your incorrect deeds and deceive yourself, others may ignore your correct deeds because they are afraid that you may betray them as you deceive yourself.

One crucial point is never to judge humans based on their appearance.

Some people are great people, and you can see this in their appearance.

At the same time, some people are not great people, but they genuinely believe that they are great people. Such people are likely to be very attractive, brave, and powerful like the great ones, but they will eventually mislead you.

262

All we do from the past to the future is to make our talents, abilities, and the true nature of our existence better.

It is an unlimited path to manifestation, not transcendence.

True transcendence is possible only in the true present moment.

You may be able to perceive a true present moment right away, or you may suddenly realize it after years of effort.

263

Our past thoughts and feelings, like a cocoon, surround us and provide us with security, but after a while, we need to let go of this small self-made world and like a butterfly fly into a vast and unlimited world.

In other words, your inner knowledge and understanding make you a butterfly, but if you can't get rid of your limited inner knowledge and understanding, you will not be able to fly into an infinite and beautiful world.

Under such circumstances, your life will become robotic and feel as if you are sleepwalking.

You will not be able to perceive the true uniqueness, greatness, and amazingness of the world, and you will eventually be buried alive in your limited world of the mind.

Your negative and positive minds and emotions are the results of the suggestions of those imprisoned in their little worlds.

Break the walls of this small, apparently massive, world and enter an incredible and indescribable world.

Behind this wall, all our hearts and souls unite in a boundless loving world -- a world of manifestation of our greatness and oneness.

Our world needs millions of great people like you instead of a few great people.

If you want to be bound by the messages of the past great men and women all your life, you have not yet understood the central message of the great men and women.

Great people like Gandhi and Martin Luther King have paved the way for us to be more transcendent human beings based on the true present moment and living facts.

264

Inner enlightenment is equal to the excellence of consciousness in a way that we can fall in love with human beings and creatures unconditionally, consciously, and unlimitedly.

265

It doesn't matter if you're a female, male, or whatever; if you want to manifest your amazing abilities and genius, respect the two aspects of your inner femininity and masculinity alike.

266

The greatest spiritual leaders in the world were not just men. I am sure the names of the majority of the world's spiritual leaders who have been women have either not been recorded or deleted from history.

In any case, to understand the truth and oneness it is not essential whether you are male or female.

Every great human being can be part of the manifestation of the truth and oneness based on his or her innate abilities and mental qualities.

The truth that has been manifested based on only a specific part of humanity cannot be complete.

267

Millions of people in the world are slaves to other humans. Hundreds of people are killed every day in some parts of the world, and I can't even talk about them. As a human being, I am ashamed wholeheartedly.

Some people believe that based on personal Karma, those people should be killed or suffer. I'm sorry for that kind of ideology.

Such a belief is the greatest insult to our humanity and the culmination of our irresponsibility.

No matter hundreds of millions of people believe in personal Karma based on good and bad; this is a human law, not a universal one.

The law of cause and effect is universal, and I accept it, but I strongly reject the personal Karma based on the good and the bad that is a kind of insult to the oneness of humans, creatures, and the world.

268

All great leaders, good or bad, are professors of self-hypnosis.

At the deepest stage of hypnosis, your eyes can be completely open and, in a state, quite like being awake. At that point, you are suggestible, like a robot, and you fall under the control of external suggestions by others.

In this state, one can open his/her eyes but does not see real things, or with open eyes s/he can see unreal things as realities according to the suggestions.

At this point, illusory spirituality may divert you from the path of pure transcendence.

Do you know what the difference between true and quasi-spirituality is?

By illusory spirituality, you are the most prominent person on earth, and you expect the whole world to serve you, but according to true spirituality, as a small part of the oneness, you unconditionally serve the world and its creatures.

269

If you can understand the oneness, you will be saddened by the problems and suffering of others, but do not imagine that your life is full of sadness. That is not true.

Understanding the oneness of your being makes you full of happiness and indescribable joy that is much more powerful and pleasant than sadness and suffering.

270

If your inner knowledge is low, you may be abused when you try to love others. Your identity will be broken, and eventually, what you think is love will become hate.

Only humans can genuinely love unconditionally, whose existence is full of inner knowledge and understanding.

Unconditional love is not just a feeling. Unconditional love is based on ever-expanding inner knowledge and understanding.

If you are a mirror that only reflects the light, the warmth, and the love of the great people, not your own, know that there are people who will consciously or unconsciously crush you.

If we think we are superior to others based on our inner knowledge and perception, we have lost our way. We must always get rid of them. The only thing that is enormously important and honorable is our oneness.

Strive to manifest the infinite source of love within yourself and, like the sun, to shine light, warmth, and love on yourself, other human beings, and creatures.

This source of love is not one person, but our oneness. When this infinite energy is activated, no one can destroy it, even the height of ignorance and hatred against it will be ineffective.

If some people think they will be able to destroy the sun of love and awareness of the oneness of humanity and the world with ignorance, prejudice, and hatred, they are entirely wrong.

One day we will see the birth of a new world -- a world where each one of us loves each other as part of our oneness with all our hearts and souls.

271

Our normal lives are based on very closely related pasts.

All these moments have passed. They were real, but unreal at the true present moment.

Accordingly, all our understanding of life, time, and existence are entirely unrealistic.

In other words, we experience death and life at the same time.

272

I can easily die in old age or young with a wealth of knowledge and experience.

This is apparently unfair! We cannot understand why so much knowledge and experience are destroyed.

Very simply I say to you, according to the truth and oneness, and the universal laws, our beliefs, knowledge, and experiences, which are based on the past, do not have true value.

In fact, there is no truth and nothing valuable except living facts based on the true present moment.

Living and fresh perceptions are far more valuable than past-based beliefs, knowledge, and experiences. This is a universal law.

Also, based on the truth and oneness and universal laws, our personal beliefs, knowledge, and experiences, which are hidden, have no actual value.

In fact, living and fresh perceptions based on our collective knowledge and experiences are valuable, not our hidden knowledge and experiences. This is also a universal law.

If you fail to manifest your thoughts, feelings, talents, and abilities, they will all be lost.

We may not like such rules, but to excel, we need to understand and coordinate ourselves with them.

273

If your thoughts, feelings, beliefs, and life are part of the oneness of humanity and the world, you will be eternal.

In other words, you will be immortal when your existence disappears in love and the oneness.

In another way, death is meaningless to one who can understand true love and the oneness.

274

Sex is a way to excellence if we meditate on the oneness and selflessness at the height of orgasm.

275

I love you. Am I better or superior to the negative people? No, being superior is just an illusion and not true.

Being superior and inferior is an ego-based mental trick.

Spiritually, no human is superior to another.

Quasi-spiritual people think they are superior or inferior to others.

True great humans can understand that every human being is a divine being, and one cannot be said to be superior or inferior to another.

Only this understanding should manifest itself in our existence.

Great people like Gandhi or Martin Luther King had realized that they were not superior to others, even people like Hitler.

They understood that the truth and oneness are beyond themselves, as good people, and oppressors and racists as bad people.

The shadow of hatred, cruelty, and racism will fade away in the light of true love.

That's their central message, which is the foundation of the oneness and unconditional love.

276

In pseudo-spirituality, your inner personality is very loose, and at the same time, your outer personality is very rigid and inflexible.

You keep your appearance, but inside you are influenced by others, so others think you are very modest.

Based on true spirituality, you can be very modest at the height of self-esteem.

Your inner personality will be powerful, but at the same time, your outer personality will be quite simple and flexible.

277

All our wise sayings are limitless mental games.

I'm always trying to show that none of these words are the reflection of the truth.

They are only a guide.

Finally, you will notice that they are useless.

Then suddenly, you will perceive the truth, and you will realize that "The truth is inexpressible."

278

I'm not talking to see cheering or praising of others. Sometimes my words are like a razor blade.

I even criticize my thoughts, beliefs, and feelings.

If you can understand unconditional love, you will realize that...

- You are not superior or inferior to other humans.
- Your country is no more important than the existence and freedom of other people.
- Your possessions and interests are no more valuable than the interests of other humans.
- Your thoughts, feelings, and beliefs are not better and more valuable than others.

There is war, crime, and cruelty in the world because we blindly love our thoughts, feelings, and beliefs.

Unconditional love means to go beyond our delusive values and to be free of our thoughts, feelings, and beliefs.

279

Sacrificing your property and body is not a sign of true love; maybe this is a suicide and an escape from life.

One can understand true love that is willing to sacrifice good and bad beliefs and thoughts and feelings for the benefit of humanity, even if others cannot understand it and will never appreciate it.

280

When you can deeper understand the suffering and pleasure of yourself and others, then you can fly better to the peaks of love and excellence.

281

Optimism is an open imagination to understanding solutions to problems that are solved through realism, but pessimism is a limited imagination to ignore the issues we want to solve solely with imagination.

282

There are various human beings and creatures in the world, and all humans have different personalities in their inner world.

However, all of this is based on the truth of oneness.

- If you are a great human being, you can understand the connection among yourself, other people, different beings, and love unconditionally.
- If you are an ordinary lover, you can only understand your relationship with another person and love him/her.
- If you are an ordinary person, you can only understand the relationship between the different personalities within you, and you are willing to sacrifice the interests of others for your ego.

- If you are crazy, you cannot understand the connection between different characters within yourself, and there is always an inner world war in your life.

283

The truth is utterly inexpressible. A belief can represent the truth if it can genuinely accept the oneness of all humanity and beings.

There is no need for fantasy and making infinite philosophies to understand the truth. These can be complex specialties or illusions that only a few people can understand, confuse the public, and have to follow them blindly because they cannot understand them.

For example, a biologist does not have to be a sociologist.

You do not need philosophy and beliefs that you cannot understand.

The truth ties our hearts together.

No matter if we are children or adults, no matter if we are illiterate or scientists, in any case, love and the oneness is the only universal truth that we can all understand and need.

284

When you are a great person, others may recognize you as a great person, but always you believe that you are an ordinary person.

If you think you are a great person and are superior to others, then be sure you do not know what greatness is.

Please go back to the ordinary lovely people before stopping yourself and others from the path to transcendence.

285

Economic and spiritual laws are not alike.

If you try to be good for the reward, and you're not bad for fear of retribution, you still don't know the difference between spirituality and economics, and this is a significant self-deception.

If your being is full of love and goodness, you will unconsciously do good and unconditionally love others. This is our true essence, and only those who spiritually mature can understand this.

286

The existence of me or others is like a mirror that each reflects a limited part of the truth.

Do not depend on this fact, as this mirror may be broken.

Forget this mirror; the primary sun of love and truth and oneness is deep within your heart and soul, where you can discover the truth of yourself, others, and me, and that is nothing but our infinite and eternal love and oneness.

287

If your inner world is like a paradise, and you feel that if others' thoughts, feelings, and beliefs are like you, the world will be like paradise, that moment knows that your path to growth and transcendence is right. Otherwise, there are drawbacks, and you must discover difficulties, fix them, and try again until your inner world becomes a true paradise.

This is beyond the pain and pleasures of the physical world.

288

The distances and boundaries between us seem to be sacred if we imagine that you and I are two separate beings.

Otherwise, our love and unity are sacred when we understand that you and I are part of the oneness.

289

When I live in a dead past, and you live in an unborn future, then based on mental experience, we feel a great distance between us.

If we can both live in the present moment, we realize that the truth of our lives is love, unity, and oneness.

290

We are ignorant, without each other's guidance and love, and ignorance is the biggest problem in human society.

Remember, it is easy for most people to love a perfect person and a lover, and it doesn't matter.

The important thing is to love weak and ignorant people and even our enemies.

Such love is very hard to express, but we need it to change our inner and outer world.

We need something beyond words so that we can truly love each other.

291

Never be sure of the truth of your thoughts, feelings, and beliefs, but rest assured that you are right if you can still love yourself and others at the height of inhuman situation and mental and emotional crisis.

292

No matter how much your wealth and assets are, in any case, you cannot understand, use, and enjoy more than your own heart and mind.

If your mind and heart are about the size of a jar, you really can't have more than one jar of water, even if you seem to own the ocean.

Instead of trying in vain to pursue the mirage of happiness based on unlimited assets and possessions, try expanding your mind and heart. How can you do that? Always learn, experience, understand the oneness, and unconditionally love yourself and others.

293

My thoughts, feelings, beliefs, my past, and the future belong to me, not you.

I cannot teach you anything even if I'm a little aware there is no expressible truth that can be said.

I am here to understand again better my connection to the oneness, including you, and to strengthen this bond.

294

When you do not understand others, you imagine that you are superior and unique, but when you can understand others, you will laugh at these illusions.

Among the billions of unique people, being special is meaningless as it is not honorable to be a star among billions of stars.

No matter who you are, if you think you are superior or inferior to me, your life path is wrong.

295

If you are humble in front of powerful people and proud in front of weak people, you are arrogant, and your life path is wrong. This is the behavior of the men or women who pretend to be great people, but they are not.

If you are proud in front of powerful people and humble in front of weak people, you are a man or woman of high self-esteem and your life path is right. It is a part of the essence and existence of true great people.

296

There is the fact that all weak human beings want to change the physical world, not their inner world.

The most important thing you can do is change your inner world, not the outer world.

If you can transform your inner world, you can be sure that it will have major and significant effects on the physical world.

In a way, we can say that you can only manifest your inner world, not your unrealistic and rootless wishes.

297

You do not need to experience true love and being great in the outside world, but to experience them within yourself.

You may be a tourist and have experienced many things, but you are not able to be a great person.

At the same time, you may be in jail but still able to be a great human being.

Great humans have a great and wonderful inner world and have experienced in their inner world many things that cannot be experienced in the outside world. These vastly different and extraordinary inner experiences make them great people.

298

The true great people are leaders of their inner world, not those who strive to be the leaders of the physical world.

The one who can be the leader of the physical world is not you or me, but our oneness.

299

Great people are those who can forgive themselves, others, and even their enemies.

300

Those who think that other humans can be their leaders will never be great.

Always remember that other great people are your friends, brothers, and sisters, and not some creatures above you.

Only those can be great people whose true leader is rooted in their hearts and souls.

301

You can influence the physical world when your inner world is better and more attractive than the outside world.

In other words, you can only manifest your inner world, not your unrealistic and rootless wishes.

The transformation and re-creation of the inner world is an art based on inner perceptions and experiences.

302

The personality of each human being is divine and valuable. Each human being has inimitable talents that are unique throughout the world.

Begging and giving money to poor people is an insult to the divine man or woman.

The true philanthropists and benefactors are those who strive to expand the centers of discovery, nurture, and support of people's talents around the world and embrace a world with open political and economic boundaries.

303

Your life is valuable and meaningful when you move along your interests, talents, and abilities.

If you are only serving the needs, interests, talents, and abilities of others, you may be rich, but your life path will be wrong and meaningless.

External wealth is a means and a necessity, but the sole purpose of your life and presence is inner wealth, which can make your life meaningful.

304

The world is not only good and bad, white, and black, but it is colorful, and life is an infinite set of colors that good and bad are just two of them.

305

Only my mind can be my biggest enemy, not other human beings.

I can love myself with all my ignorance and mistakes while I can hurt myself more than anyone else.

So, there is no reason not to love other humans and creatures.

306

Knowing is like reading and learning to describe the water's properties in the book without experiencing water.

Understanding means experiencing the water with all the senses and directly try to understand instead of knowing.

Our world is full of people who are scientists, scholars, and experts about love and humanity but who have never been able to understand the oneness, true love, and true humanitarian values.

They are like children who teach sexology while never having sex.

Only those who truly can understand love and humanity are those who are spiritually and emotionally mature.

True love is the result of spiritual and emotional maturity, as orgasm is the result of sexual maturity.

307

Our minds and hearts are filled with illusions that are more important to us than facts -- illusions that we cannot easily refute or prove.

If we think and feel more impartially and realistically, we will be able to understand that there are universal unity and connection between us.

Only in such a situation, our life can be based on unconditional love.

308

Our path to excellence is wrong if we think that our divine, human, personal thoughts, feelings, and beliefs are more important than the lives of others.

309

When there is infinite freedom, peace, and paradise in your inner world, but your physical environment is minimal, full of hatred and like Hell, then you have to have immense spiritual power to be able to handle the pressure of two very different worlds and protect your inner world and love unconditionally.

However, living in these conditions is not an honor, and you are not always right.

310

I imagine a world in which none of us are equal, but each of us is accepted as a unique being, and at the same time, we have an equal right to choose to create our lives based on our talents, interests, and abilities.

311

Some people's conditions are like those who are trapped in a deep well. We pass by the well and hear the voices of the people inside the well.

Instead of helping the people inside the well, we say to them, "This is your destiny, calm down to die in peace."

If we misuse concepts such as peace and tranquility in the path of irresponsibility, our spirituality is a great self-deception.

If we believe in separation and cannot unconditionally serve and help others, our spirituality is just a profound illusion to deceive ourselves and others.

312

Where stupid, fanatical, and selfish people are rich and powerful, and humanitarian, intelligent, and kind-hearted people are slaves, death is better than life.

313

When there are significant obstacles in your path, you must have ambitious goals in life.

In such a situation, you will have the motivation and power to resist the enormous obstacles and problems and eventually get rid of them; otherwise, your life and death may be useless.

Always remember that you may not achieve most of your realistic goals unless you have much larger and more idealistic goals in a way that opens up your mind and heart enough to be able to reach your realistic goals.

314

When you feel the possibility of death and your eyes are forced to open, you realize that there is nothing more valuable than helping and serving others along the path of love and humanity.

All your power, wealth, and selfishness will become a mirage in a moment, and great remorse will engulf your whole being.

Our true identity lies in two things:

1. When we change our inner world according to our talents, interests, and abilities, we make it better and more beautiful.

2. When we can serve others based on our inner world, and with our activities can be a model in the path of creating a better and more beautiful world.

Most people know a lot about love, but they cannot understand its truth.

Great people can understand that the need to love and be loved unconditionally is the most valuable thing in life that is deeply common in the depth of our being, and true love is the most potent force in the world for coordination and connection among people and creatures, manifestation of oneness and the creation of miracles and wonders.

Just as anyone cannot create beautiful masterpiece paintings, in the same way, everyone cannot harmonize and make beautiful their inner world, except at the peak of manifestation of their unique talents and abilities.

Creating a beautiful, harmonious, free, and wonderful inner world is the most significant and most prestigious art we can learn in a lifetime. It is a super-art based on the art of loving oneself and others, truly and unconditionally.

318

A humanitarian sometimes has to sacrifice many of his/her interests for others. Others think s/he has lost something, and they have benefited.

However, in the end, we will all find out that the real benefit lies in our heart feelings and our being quality, neither in our possessions nor in the minds which we used to deceive ourselves.

319

We are not here to torment ourselves and do everything to earn unlimited money and eventually enjoy a better house, car, and facilities for a short time in life.

We are here to live and work based on our talents, interests, and abilities, and to enjoy the opportunities and blessings of life at any moment together.

320

The path to growth in life is far more important than the goals of life.

We are mistaken if we think that achieving goals, regardless of being positive or negative, equals happiness.

Goals only determine the course of our lives.

Achieving goals in every way, positive or negative, is not worthwhile.

In fact, no matter what our goals are, goals that are not symbolic of moving in the right direction are worthless.

In other words, our goals must move us on the path of life to our growth and service to others; otherwise, our goals will be just a mirage of happiness.

Someday we will realize that our fleeting pleasures are based on goals, but the secret to true happiness and a meaningful life lies in moving in the right direction.

321

Your romantic and positive thoughts and words are like ordinary light. They may be able to warm you and others a little bit, but they usually cannot change your existence or your life.

However, romantic, positive emotions and deeds are like the focused sunlight under the magnifying glass and will change the life of yourself and others as much as possible.

322

Worthwhile goals that give meaning to your life are valuable even behind obstacles.

In demanding situations, ordinary people replace alternative, easy-to-use, and worthless goals to the main goals and destroy their true identity. They think that achieving false goals can satisfy them, but in the end, they will realize that their goals were just a mirage of happiness.

Great men and women cannot think of anything other than their original goals, even if many of their common interests are destroyed, and their efforts fail thousands of times.

Such people usually achieve their goals, but even if they fail, they will eventually find out that they have lived honestly for genuine values and worthwhile goals, and that will be the reason to feel meaning and satisfaction in their hearts and souls.

Great people can understand that the secret to true happiness and a meaningful life lies in moving in the right direction of life and in actual goals, not in the pursuit of false targets.

323

A great man or woman is not one who wants to have the best things, but someone who wants to be the best person that can give others the best things.

324

Sometimes, I criticize some of your thoughts, words, and deeds.

It doesn't mean I don't love you, because at the same time, I am the greatest critic of my mistakes, and still, I can love and let myself grow up in the path of transcendence and oneness.

You are still the loving human being, which is a part of my being, even if our ignorance and mistakes sometimes are painful.

Someday you'll understand that our love, oneness, and happiness are more valuable than anything, precisely more than everything we think, feel, do, or have.

325

Some people do not know what the difference between arrogant and self-respecting people is.

Arrogant people are proud of what they have. They humiliate themselves in front of more prosperous and more powerful people and are kind to them while maintaining and enhancing what they have, and at the same time, consider themselves superior to the poor and weak people, and they are unkind towards them.

But self-respecting people are proud of who they are. They do not consider themselves superior or inferior and do not need the approval of others. They are strong in the face of powerful people, and they are humble in the face of the weak ones. They also try to be kind to everyone, but they are more kind to needy people.

326

If you decide to close your eyes, no one can help you to see the light. In such a situation, even the sunlight is not enough to see what's existing and near you.

You can never truly accept and love someone as they are; if your love, loyalty, honesty, and forgiveness are easily lost because your beloved is not perfect.

327

The person who you are is based on a reflection of your true beliefs, not your illusions, mental errors, and deceptions, and the truth is beyond your true beliefs.

328

I'm here to tell you, my way and belief are mine, and maybe wrong or meaningless in your life.

Don't follow me and others, but only follow your own inner guide. Only follow the way and the things you love in the depth of your heart.

Finally, our souls will bring us to a point at the height of love and oneness.

329

We don't need to try to be a special person according to others, but we should discover and manifest the special one who we are, and what we want in the depth of our hearts.

330

Ultimately, we will know that all our successes would be nothing more than a mirage, and we will die for nothing if we cannot protect our dreams and follow our hearts.

Our happiness and inner paradise are based on the manifestation of the special one who we are genuinely beside each other, not the things we can have, far away from each other.

331

The things we can obtain are the instruments that we need to use them and make our inner music resonates in the world.

332

If your inner world is not at peace, the cruelty and violence of others can become part of your inner world, and you will lose your resistance to adverse conditions, and it makes you crumble.

333

Destiny is not an unchangeable truth. Destiny is a predictable future based on our beliefs and boundaries of mind and heart.

For great people who continually expand the boundaries of their beliefs, minds, and hearts, a global destiny is meaningful, and individual destiny is meaningless.

334

The sun is continuously the sun, even at the back of the moon. A great human being is always a great human being, even in the depths of a dungeon.

Great women and men are those who can be freed from incorrect values and beliefs and love unconditionally at the height of physical and social limitations, problems, obstacles, hatred, and crime.

335

Activities and responsibilities are what we have. They do not represent who we indeed are. The oneness of you and me is the only truth we are.

Only when we believe that our relationships and oneness are more important than our work and activities, then we can have a happy global family for a lifetime.

336

There are no innocent people in the world.

Great men and women are those who may be led astray for the short-term, but will soon correct themselves, while other people still think, they are innocent.

337

Great men and women are always looking for a positive point in your heart and soul to forget your negative points, but others still want to find a negative point in your behavior and speech to ignore all your goodness.

Unconditional love is the art of great people.

338

Life is not only black and white but also colorful, and the problems and misunderstandings are only a small part of it.

There are people who, at the height of the problems, can still understand happiness and unconditionally love others.

Such people embrace life in all its colors, so they can see the true design of this masterpiece of creation and move on the path of excellence.

339

True spirituality does not say that I am separate from you, and my ego as a reward for my goodness can become a voluptuary of the metaphysical world.

True spirituality is transcendence in the way we understand that we are an infinite, living, and magnificent oneness, and there is no boundary between us.

Those who have had such an experience know the best reward is to understand that we need no compensation because love and goodness are just a reflection of our existence, nothing else.

340

Those who move on the path of growth and transcendence are much more likely to experience failure, difficulties, and obstacles than others, while at the same time, enjoy success, happiness, peace, and freedom more than others.

341

True spirituality is not a slave to any political or economic system.

342

True spirituality is not based on financial generosity. Humans need our love and attention more than our money.

The generosity of rich people is a good thing, but not a reason for their greatness.

Great people are those who care and love others unconditionally.

343

Killings of people and other crimes around the world are based on the collective global KARMA, not personal Karma.

Most criminals need our love and attention to understand who they are in the depth of their souls and learn the correct way to live.

We think we are innocent, but it's not true. All of us, including me, are responsible for all the crimes, even if we were not involved directly.

344

All beings in the depths of their existence are directly related to each other, and this is where we are all one.

True spirituality is not having positive or not having negative thoughts, speech, or deeds based on certain beliefs, but understanding this oneness.

345

There is no evil force in the world, but our ignorance and incompatibility with natural law and universal Karma.

There is no war between the subjective forces of good and evil.

There are two basic principles in the physical world:

1. Knowledge or lack of knowledge, light, or absence of light.

2. Harmonization or lack of alignment with natural and universal laws

And in true spirituality, all the meanings of good and evil, light and darkness become meaningless, and there is nothing but love and oneness.

346

There is no place more sacred than your heart when love and oneness manifest there, beyond your gender and your beliefs.

347

Are my beliefs and words based on the truth?

The answer is straightforward. Yes, if there is not my ego, me and what is mine, to ask.

348

Others cannot impose their beliefs on you if you are not a prisoner of your ego, but part of the oneness.

This is the only way to manifest freedom in the depths of your hearts and soul and discover the truth.

349

True spirituality does not mean building and strengthening a spiritual ego to have fun in a spiritual world and ignore the suffering of others.

True spirituality is sharing our hearts and souls based on unconditional love to serve human beings and creatures that are part of our oneness.

350

Our true home is in each other's hearts.

It doesn't matter how much we are rich based on our houses or accounts.

In any case, we are always displaced, if we still didn't find our true home and those who are waiting for us in their hearts.

351

Your life meaning is in the path of inner peace, love, and truth, not based on what you have and may lose at any moment.

352

If there is the truth, it is universal and equal for all human beings and creatures.

So, if there is a belief that connects all of us, it can be based upon "the truth." Otherwise, it is just a reality based on our subjective imagination, and we need to deceive ourselves into believing it rather than "the truth."

353

The truth is not a belief that can change or be lost, but something that is part of you forever.

The belief I have learned is a reality, not the truth.

354

Something that can be visualized may be a reality, but it is not the truth.

The truth manifests itself when our imagination and beliefs stop as unconditional love and oneness will come true when our ego disappears.

355

The truth is not what you think or believe, but what we feel as one.

There is not "the truth" if you can imagine it.

356

We are an infinite oneness with different avatars.

357

The greatest human crimes have been in the name of what we believe to be sacred, while they are the greatest obstacle to love and unity between us.

358

There is an illusion in our minds, and we think that there is a great and true purpose that we can achieve without the need for others, but the truth is that there are no great goals except our oneness.

One day we will regret why we left each other alone while we were part of the key to happiness and understanding the truth.

359

A spiritual man or woman is not a person who has no emotions, but someone who can lead and manage her/his pain and pleasure, and good and bad feelings. Such a person is not a slave to the sensations and situations, even if her/his body is a slave of physical limitations temporarily.

360

Ordinary people seek to achieve big goals based on the belief of others in the world, but great men and women seek to discover and manifest their true identity in life.

361

Our beliefs are illusions, and not the truth until we can understand our oneness deep within us.

There is no indirect way to discover the truth, and you can never understand the truth if you follow the words of others or a book (including my book).

Only our inner guide can tell us the truth deep inside of us, where we are all one and the borders among you, and all the mediators and I are meaningless.

362

The life of those who are in poor conditions, but they hope for better conditions in the future is more meaningful and enjoyable than the life of those who are in excellent condition and expect nothing better.

363

The reality is like a corpse, and the truth is its aliveness.

True love is not a feeling based on different stable, old, and dead facts and values. Rather, it is a hyper-consciousness based on a refreshing truth, which is on the basis of the universal oneness that is new at every moment.

The secret of the meaning of life and happiness lies in true love that is always alive in the transcendental moments and free from physical appearance.

364

You will become a slave to an absurd and repetitive life with a pleasing outlook if you follow the old facts, speech, beliefs, and values of others to discover the truth.

The truth only manifests deep within us when we are all one, and the words like I and you and also all the middlemen are pointless.

365

Brave people are not those who do everything to gain more power and wealth, but those who pursue their desires and goals.

Achieving great goals based on the beliefs and values of others is just an illusion of happiness.

True happiness is based on discovering and manifesting your true identity and living a life filled with love and peace.

366

Fate does not say that you must be miserable, hapless, and unhappy.

Destiny says you have unique talents and abilities, and you must strive to manifest your true self to have a meaningful and valuable life; and if necessary, in your whole life, try to discover your original truth and promote your values. Otherwise, if you follow the values of others, no wealth or power can be meaningful to your life. And your fate will be out of your hands.

367

You can only get rid of negative emotions when you are not captive to your positive emotions.

Then your soul is mature enough that the unconditional love manifests in your life, and in the depths of your existence, you will experience lovemaking with the oneness of creatures and the universe.

When you become physically mature, you realize what sex is, and you can't understand it before, even if you know a lot about it.

Likewise, until you become spiritually mature, you will not be able to understand true love and oneness.

You cannot find the truth in any book, even these words I present to you.

Our spiritual words are based solely on a mental game to describe something that is not the .truth. They are like encrypted messages whose true concepts can be decrypted deep within you.

The appearance concepts of these words can only give you the insight to understand what the truth is not.

Otherwise, no words can tell you the truth, but everything is deep within you, and you need to find the true concepts.

Spiritual maturity opens your inner eyes, and lets you see the one who can be part of your happiness, among the billions of people.

This inner awareness is an introduction to the manifestation of true happiness.

370

A great man or woman is the one who laughs at his or her problems in the most challenging moments in life and is someone who believes that s/he cannot be a slave of barriers and limitations so that everything will be okay.

371

Our talents and abilities are the most important things that we have, and being the person who is filled with inner peace beside the one who accepts and loves us unconditionally is the most valuable thing that we can be.

372

Listening to your inner voice is wisdom, and the ability to hear the voice of another heart is divinity.

373

I'm dreaming of a day that our hearts will be intermediaries between our interests, not political and economic systems, and I imagine the day that our love is a measure for our valuableness instead of money and power.

We laugh at this ambition today, and future generations will laugh at our fanaticism for the false values.

Great people are those whose physical location and time cannot limit their souls, hearts, and minds. Otherwise, they can never be a great man or woman.

374

The criterion of the truth is love. Otherwise, there is no truth, and you will be lost in many philosophies and theories for something that does not exist.

375

We cannot perceive our oneness if the essential things in our life are "me" and "you" or "mine" and "yours."

376

There are not enough reasons for Karma based on possible past and future lives, and this belief is generally based on a set of theories.

From my point of view, we are all one oneness like an ocean. At some point in time, we appear like separated droplets. After this manifestation, we are again bound to the ocean of oneness; and yet, at another time, other drops may appear. The process will continue.

These new droplets may be part of us, but they may not be precisely those previous drops. So, if we can understand something called our past life, it may be part of one's, or other's experiences, that part of our existence is shared with him or her based on oneness. However, there is no reason to prove that we are the same person or being, but with a new life and form.

It should be noted that the drop is a metaphor for one's soul and consciousness, not one's body.

When one experiences inner illumination, she or he realizes the oneness, and at this moment, the ego is entirely meaningless. The person after this transcendence will not be the same, even if her or his whole body is the same. It is a kind of self-conscious death and a revival in the form of a new ego that belongs to the whole and to reflect oneness.

In a natural death, this is unconscious. The current ego dies, and a different ego forms at separate times and places. That is different from the thing or person that exists now, even with a different body and form.

When we believe in unity, in fact, there is nothing separate whose good and bad are completely unique to itself.

As the oneness, we all share and are responsible for the badness of others, just as others share in our goodness.

Goodness and badness are relative things for one person and have different meanings and interpretations in different situations and cultures and regions and times.

Global Karma is completely verifiable, but personal Karma based on the separation of every creature from others is just a relative fact that varies across conditions and regions of the world.

For example, precisely two good people, one in North Korea and the other in Denmark cannot have the same fate. Just like a person who lived in Germany during World War II and someone grows up in present-day Germany, their future and Karma are not the same, even if they are twin flames.

377

The discussion of reincarnation and Karma can be hugely different based on biology, psychology, religion, philosophy, and spirituality.

In my opinion, reincarnation can be a spiritual evolution, but according to the laws of biology, while, for me, spirituality and oneness have a different meaning.

As I mentioned earlier, I believe in universal Karma and reincarnation, but not personal reincarnation and Karma.

I talked to people many years ago, who have had different experiences. For example, one person had experienced that he was another person a hundred years ago or one million years ago he was a sludge under the sea, and so on.

It is easy to understand such an experience with psychoanalysis through hypnosis, and I saw this experience in others many years ago.

There is something called the collective unconscious, and some people can understand something about the past or future possibilities, and I can't deny it.

I'm not talking about physical evidence. If we judge on this basis, there is much evidence to support any religion or doctrine as the truth -- something that is not correct.

Experiences, knowledge, and age are within the realm of reality and not a measure of the truth.

The laws of spirituality and biology are not alike, and in the spiritual aspect, a plant or an animal is complete and is part of the manifestation of oneness that it doesn't need to evolve.

In my opinion, the spiritual journey is something different from the understanding of oneness.

In spiritual exploration, there are various stages and specific times and places in an inner world infinitely more than the physical world. Evolution is a theory based on an infinite path whose end is not known, and so, I said that personal Karma is a theory.

This "me" and "you" is a fictitious ego-based concept, while both can be two faces of the oneness.

I cannot believe that I can achieve universal oneness without others.

The number of living things has been increasing over time, and there is no reason to be the same as what they were a million years ago and now.

What do we mean by perfection, knowledge, and experiences? It is clear that a baby is without these things, so how can this evolution continue with death and birth?

The oneness manifests itself when all levels, time, place, and entity become meaningless.

There is no separation, and the need for time and place for the evolution of the soul is meaningless because we are not talking about a physical journey.

I have already mentioned the understanding of a prior life that "if we can understand something under the name of our past life, it may be part of the experience of another person" or creatures whom part of their and our existence were/are shared based on the oneness."

To me, global Karma is a law like the law of cause and effect, but personal Karma is a theory like quantum mechanics. For example, we experience many things based on Einstein's relativity or quantum physics, but these are still theories and were not accepted as scientific laws. However, in the future, according to new evidence, it is possible to be accepted as scientific laws or to remain only as theories.

Scientifically if there is something that we have some reasons to prove it, and yet there are some reasons to reject it, it is a theory.

Many religions and doctrines believe in reincarnation and personal Karma, yet their definitions are vastly different about reincarnation and Karma. There is much criticism; on the other hand, that's why I call it a theory.

Also, what I have said based on my experiences is a theory, and the truth is not something that can be expressed in words. I trust my personal inner experience, but I do not trust the words and mental meanings, which are a factor for separation and an obstacle to understanding the oneness.

Also, I have not rejected personal Karma, but consider it relative. What I reject is the constant and absolute personal Karma.

Where we have an equal right to choose the way of life, personal Karma is a reality, but it is still dependent on universal Karma. Where there is no equal right to choose, personal Karma is very pale, and universal Karma is very vibrant.

There are many questions about this.

Where have you and I been for billions of years before all beings came into being? Is there a reason we were separate spirits? Have we all been an imperfect spirit to need perfection? If we were not perfect as pure spirit, how can we achieve perfection in the always incomplete human and physical form?

What I have experienced is that the "I" is a mental image based on the temporal body and physical world and not the truth of my being. Our souls are fully interconnected; they are not independent; they are parts of our spirit. Our true spirit and being are one and complete and do not need perfection. We need to understand this so that we can step in the direction of manifestation of the oneness, not a continuous movement in the path of oneness.

From my own spiritual experience, I have come to realize that the purpose of our life in this world is not perfection, but an understanding of the oneness and striving to manifest it in numerous ways based on our unique natural and inherent blessings.

378

Ordinary people have variable and superficial goals, and their approaches to achieve them are fixed and inflexible.

Great men and women have fixed goals, and their ways to achieve them are flexible.

379

It is not sacred, but a deviation from spirituality. If we have a belief that is a barrier for our oneness, and especially when we believe that this belief is more important than people's lives.

380

Great people can never forget their goals and dreams, even in the worst conditions, because a human being who likes and accepts to live under the imposed goals and values by others is practically an immature person who cannot be great.

381

The world is not black and white but colored.

In the same way, people are not just good or bad.

Goodness and badness are merely relative concepts based on our subjective judgment, and such things do not exist in nature.

Believing in good and evil has been the biggest reason to justify the greatest crimes in the history of humanity.

We never can love unconditionally until the moment we can forget goodness and badness and accept people as divine creatures who may make mistakes in their lives.

382

True love and the truth are always two lights from one source.

True love cannot be stopped, as the truth cannot be destroyed by our thoughts, words, and actions --both are parts of our true existence when they manifest and light up our inner world.

383

Some people may ask who are the criminals if we do not have bad people?

The answer is simple -- they are extremely sick people physically, psychologically, and emotionally. Their way of life should not be our model, but the news about their actions as great men or women shall be stopped, and, they must be limited and should be under care and treatment.

Their negative energy will disappear if they notice that there is nobody who cares and pays attention to their inappropriate behaviors.

Our way must be based on love and philanthropy if we are healthy people.

384

If we always share wise words of others, we will not be able to understand their mistakes and shortcomings, and we will build our life upon imperfect perceptions without understanding the true concepts behind their words.

Find and share your inner wisdom. Be a direct intermediary between the pure wisdom and divinity and not be only a loudspeaker for the sound of other great men or women.

385

Sometimes you cannot explain the truth that you understand, and you are upset that you cannot transfer your perception and experience to those whom you love, especially when they are repeating the mistakes that you have experienced.

The words, logic, and philosophy are useless in such circumstances. They may need to experience that way to be sure that way is wrong.

Just be kind, love unconditionally, and be ready to help them in the difficulties and problems.

Finally, patience and pure love can light up their path to show them what is the correct way, and the fact that they have a better way to choose.

386

Choose "the truth," if you must choose between "love" and "the truth," because the "love" you see may not be matched to "the truth," while "the truth" and "true love" always matches.

387

We know that we must live in the "here and now."

Great people and ordinary people, both live based on the fact, but what is the difference between them?

Ordinary people live based on values, conditions, and limitations of the location and region where their bodies are there, and according to the time that they are experiencing.

However, for great people, "now" is the moment that their true nature is shining, and "here" is where their heart is, and also their ideas can come true.

In other words, they live in the "here" and "now" beyond space and time constraints.

388

Someone who only reflects your strengths may not be a person who loves you truly; unless he or she lets you face your weaknesses at the same time, and help you to fix them and grow up in the best way possible.

389

Your best partner is someone who, as a clean mirror, shows you your strengths and weaknesses.

Additionally, she or he is someone who shows you and others their strengths to further strengthen them, and show you in private, your weaknesses, and helps you to fix them.

390

A true and permanent relationship is based on full awareness of each other's strengths and weaknesses.

It is doomed to failure, the common life that is merely based on strengths, and lovers hide one another's weaknesses from each other, and cannot accept each other unconditionally with all their strengths and weaknesses.

391

You may be scared to get close to another heart and soul indefinitely when you cannot understand true love. When you do not understand the oneness, and you think this is a kind of slavery, it terrifies you because you should try to lose for oneness, the false self, the ego, and the identity that society has suggested to you.

You can experience oneness, infinite and true nature, freedom, and independence in your inner world only when you have enough courage to lose the false self and let the masks fade away.

392

No man or woman is holy unless the moment oneness manifests in their hearts and souls beyond femininity and masculinity.

393

Great men and women are never "the second person" in life, but they become the great people whom no one in the world can replace.

How? With recognition, development, promotion, and protection of their original identity and true nature as a unique human being in the world.

394

In general, each of us is talented in certain areas, and this is usually part of our genetics. This is something that was determined with our birth and without our authority.

However, we have the power to try to determine the type and direction of our life based on our talents, abilities, and interests.

Fate is something we can create ourselves, of course, within a specific range; otherwise, others will determine our destiny.

Finding your certain ranges and moving along that path means touching inner freedom and pristine experience of the true meaning of being and life.

This is the introduction for your ability to unconditionally love yourself and others.

395

Many people in the world glow like scattered candles, and their luminosity is based on the continuity of darkness. When the sun of love and truth rises, the light of all the candles disappears.

396

When you are following your inner guide, ultimately, you want to say something inexpressible.

It will be the moment that you have no choice, but you have to try to show it by your deeds, to say something that there is no word to explain it.

This is the first step to manifest a great evolution in your inner world.

397

A tiny piece of a diamond can be priced equal to thousands of tons of crystals.

Similarly, there are humans that one moment of their presence is more valuable than living a lifetime with other people.

398

Inner illumination is not an abnormal experience, but a moment of complete harmony between the soul and the psyche and emotions with the universe and physical reality, in other words, a moment of perfect harmony and connection between the inner and outer worlds.

Inner illumination is a manifestation of the moment when the boundary between our inner and outer world has been removed, and we can understand the oneness and unity of the whole being and the universe.

399

Watch divinely and act like a human.

400

No man or woman, contrary to their imagination, needs to get the attention of others by doing bad and good acts; on the contrary, every person's need is to get the attention of herself/himself and to respect and care for herself/himself.

401

The truth cannot be understood by force on oneself and others because someone who uses power to make sense of it is either unjustified, or they do not have the information and reason to prove it right. Someone who, because of his/her pride and fanaticism, refuses to investigate the matter to prove it calmly, it should be noted that the use of force to prove the truth will destroy its value to himself/herself and others.

402

The greatest creativity of spiritual people is to create their divine personalities.

403

People who are frustrated with life, about opportunities they have similar reactions and actions, means they are apathetic, but those who love life and the world have a balanced response to anything that fits it.

404

The real art is not to make ordinary things with excellent equipment. Instead, the real skill is to create better and quality things with minimal possibilities and to discover the most valuable things.

A true artist is someone who strives to maximize knowledge and understanding as well as expand his or her abilities and powers to create a lasting masterpiece.

405

The truth is what it is. It is not come and go, but the reality is something that comes and goes.

406

The patience is not to suppress our emotions and to accept oppression, but to maintain peace in all our work and to strengthen our resistance.

407

It is impossible to reform the world except by a lack of focusing on the differences and creating a heartfelt unification of different cultures and races.

408

If one does not understand something, he/she is not responsible for it, and should not be held accountable for something he/she cannot understand. If one does not have the right to choose equality, he/she has no equal responsibility.

409

The value of a person is not based on the services and goods they use, but on the type of goods and services that each produces and offers.

410

There is a super-conscious divine power in the universe, but this is by far extremely different from the God of religions. The world is governed by the rules of that divine power, which is based on harmony and disharmony.

411

It would be best if you did everything you can do to solve your problem when there is an emergency.

However, most of the time there is no emergency; but you have bad feelings. In this situation, do not plan, do not say a word, and do not do anything; hide yourself from others, lay down, breath deep, and imagine you are someone else who is only watching another one's pain and suffering, not yours as if a movie and a story that is not real.

And after a long time that you practice in this way, you will realize those bad feelings are like a sea, and you have learned to control yourself and swim in your feelings and get out sooner and better, instead of drowning in them and losing the value and meaning of your life.

412

If you were not reading good books or were not watching inspirational videos, your life and feelings could be terrible. Sometimes your thoughts and feelings make deep and strong roots for a long time; then you will be realized that you made a good situation to act and grow.

413

You have the divine power of creation of everything you can imagine clearly in your mind the same way you see reality.

The purity and quality of your love and freedom determine how much you can create your imaginations.

414

We have many emotions like joy, passion, pleasure, sadness, anger, pain, and suffering. None of them are stable, but they are always changing like clouds.

The emotions are deceiving us, and they cover our eyes and awareness of the truth.

Love is not an emotion, but the quality of our being.

Once you are above the clouds of emotions, a moment manifests, and you are witness to who you are and the love that is stable and always present, like the sky.

415

It seems most of the people are living in the "here and now," but their awareness, feelings, and thoughts are about the past and the future. Living in the "now and here" means you are aware of who and what you are and what is the manifestation of your existence for now and here.

For example, if you are a singer, living in the "here and now" means forgetting the past, future and even yourself, and manifest as a pure song. Then it can touch other's hearts and create a fantastic effect.

Living in the "here and now" means being at the level of a pure love, which whatever you do comes from the depths of your hearts and souls, and it manifests as a brilliant effect of your authentic presence and existence when erupting with pure nature of love.

416

The dark world of hatred and deception is something fake created by the people who follow the wrong values. However, there are still many great people with kind hearts and shining souls who are scattered like bright candles around the world. You are one of them, and I am no one, but only a mirror that shows you this truth.

The main problem is that the great people are scattered like stars in the infinite darkness. I hope that one day, these lights come together united and as a centralized society in a point of the world to shine like one sun, and to warm the frozen conscience of the people of other societies and awake their awareness. This can be the starting point for the manifestation of a new culture based on unconditional love, and also, the transformation of the path of evolution of humankind.

417

Our subconscious mind has been indirectly programmed from childhood by believing in wrong values and following specific systems. We are somehow conditioned that unconsciously pleased with optional and collective bondage.

Sacred slavery, with the cover of legal and beautiful names! For example, the economic system was for valuing goods and services. That's what it seems to be.

However, the truth is that it is a system for valuing humans, which can be sometimes direct and sometimes indirect.

There is an international show that inspires us in which the value of human beings is determined in accordance with human rights law. This is one of the same programmings for your subconscious mind.

The truth is that the political and economic systems determine our value as human beings, and based on the interests of the same methods, it can change.

True freedom and your actual value are what is in your hands and is not something others can increase or decrease to control you like slaves and dolls.

Drafting of the Universal Declaration of Human Rights was one of the honors of the human community.

The problem has started since the political and economic systems interpreted it according to their interests.

Many humanitarian and human rights organizations work under the supervision of economic and political systems. What they do is an international show, and frequently, they close their eyes to the truth and genuine human values given the interests of the political and economic systems even in non-free countries. This is one of the main reasons for not solving the significant problems of human society.

If there is still goodness in this world, it is due to the existence of people who committed to love and philanthropy and unconditional human rights, regardless of what the interests of economic and political systems are.

Maybe some of those people cooperate with humanitarian and human rights organizations, but without a doubt, the vast majority of them operate outside any system and organization because they live the loving being who they are, not to make a show for others or to have political and financial benefits.

When true and pure love manifests, your belief system breaks down.

Our life is like a painting masterpiece that we create.

Our belief systems have suggested to us that there is in the world, either goodness or badness -- black and white.

Our life is not only black and white, but there are many things, thoughts, feelings, and experiences in our lives that are neither black nor white, but waver in different spectrums. However, because of our belief system, we like to classify them within the two categories: black (bad) and white (good).

Sometimes, in different times, places, and conditions, the black thing which is bad for us will be turned into white (good), or vice versa.

In fact, the truth cannot change. Something that is really black (bad) should be black (bad) at any time and place, and it is the same about white (good).

If their places change in our category, it's not because the truth is changing, but because our categorization is limited, and we incorrectly categorized something as bad or good -- something that is neither black nor white.

To create the masterpiece of our own lives, we have to see black and white in their places. Also, we need to increase our perception beyond black and white to understand hundreds of other colors of life and to use them in their places to create the masterpiece of our lives.

Once our perception goes beyond the black (bad) and white (good), we can see all the colors of life in their places. This is the moment that we can love something/someone purely and truly.

The black and white are concepts to express the quality of our attitude toward good and bad; and not any physical color. The physical white and black colors are some things that are neither good nor bad.

420

Generosity to others is a natural part of our life, the same way that breathing is.

As we do not expect anyone to thank us for exhalation of breath, in the same way, there is no need to expect anyone to thank us for our generosity.

True generosity shines as part of our being, like the sunshine, and it is not something that we decide to show or not, the same way you do not choose to breathe if you are alive.

Someone may not be generous but has a different positive talent and trait. It is important to let shine our original being, not to fake something, only because others believe it is better.

421

No matter who I am or not, my view and perception are one in 7.7 billionths of human society (at the time of publishing this book). I only can see the truth of my inner world that is only one aspect of the Universal Truth.

All of us need to find our inner truth. Each one can manifest one of the aspects of the Universal Truth.

They will be like pieces of a global puzzle -- none of them are perfect, but together and in their right places can complete the global puzzle.

Only then can we witness the masterpiece of the Universal Truth at the moment of the reunification of our inner consciousness and the global consciousness.

Out of that moment, there is no way to express or to understand the Universal Truth by words or shows.

The Universal Truth is not something one or more people can dictate, say, or show you.

The truth-seekers are not the ones who try to be the leader of others to dictate, say, or show them imaginations about the truth under the name of the Universal Truth.

You can go even higher than your university professor. The same way the great men and women educate you to seek and find your inner truth and go higher, not to follow them as kids forever.

422

I do not share anything which others like to hear or see, but only something that I want to transfer from my inner world to the outer world.

The sun does not shine because we need it, and the flowers are not beautiful because we like to see them. Nature is valuable only because of its trueness that manifests unconditionally.

The peak of life is to be aware of your true being, as it is, and only enjoy its expression and manifestation with no reason and no reward.

We are looking for a reward only when what we say or do is fake and does not come from the depth of our being.

Something that is not important for us, but we need an excuse to believe it is valuable and enjoyable.

It is fake happiness when you try to enjoy something that others suggest is valuable and enjoyable, but you cannot feel satisfaction deep inside your heart and soul.

True happiness means enjoying the natural aliveness of your true being, and anything that comes up from the inner truth.

423

Human beings commit suicide in three states of mind:

1. When the inner and outer worlds of "ignorant and weak people" both become a Hell.

2. When the outer world of "successful and wealthy people" is like Heaven, but their inner world is like a Hell.

3. When the inner world of "great people" is like paradise, but the outer world becomes Hell for them to the extent that it can destroy the values and beauty of their inner world. They feel they must cut their communication bridge to the outer world before they have to abandon their sublime values and change their identities in favor of inhuman powers. In fact, this is the highest form of sacrifice to protect humanity in the worst possible circumstances, for the truth they lived for and are also willing to die for.

True happiness manifests at the moment your inner world is beautified, and you can open the gates of your inner world to the outer world to move and live originally, purely and freely.

424

Since childhood, until now, you have always tried to make your clothes fit for your body, and not your body fit for the clothes you like.

Your thoughts, feelings, and beliefs are like the clothes, and you need to fit them for the human being who you are now, not to fit yourself and your life for them.

425

Imagine, at one point of the world, there are 20,000,000,000,000,000,000,000,000 (twenty sextillions) pebbles.

There are very tiny creatures on one of the pebbles.

The creatures divided the pebble among themselves, and they agreed to limit each other to have one part and not to enter the various parts of the pebble; otherwise, they should be killed or suffer.

Think that you are a human being and billions of times greater than the tiny creatures.

What do you think about what they do on one pebble?

Do you think those creatures are wise?

Maybe you wonder what some of those tiny creatures say to others that they know the absolute truth, not only about their pebble but about humans and the whole world!

Do you believe them?

Do you follow them?

It is estimated that we have 20 sextillions (20,000,000,000,000,000,000,000,000) planets in the observable universe, and earth is one of them.

The way we think, do, and believe in this planet is like the tiny creatures.

Wake up! The truth of your being is much higher than the little thoughts and beliefs and deeds.

If you believe that future generations of humanity will think that we were wise people, then think again!

426

There is nothing in nature to try to become or show something else that is not, but everything manifests itself as it is.

For example, a flower does not grow to become a tree or to make you happy. There is no purpose. It is beautiful and can make you happy, only because it is original, not because it had any goal to make you happy or to make itself attractive. The value is based on its originality.

We think the purpose of life is to achieve extraordinary things, knowledge, and abilities that we do not have, but if they are the goal of life, how can death take all of them from us, and sometimes before we enjoy what we achieved?

Because the law of nature and the universe is different from what we think, the purpose of life is the manifestation and flourishing of our true existence based on the original talents and interests we have.

The purpose of life is all about the manifestation of your originality, not to fake another person who is not you truly.

427

Ordinary people think their beliefs are the truth.

Great men and women do not believe their beliefs are the truth, but they open their minds, heart, and soul to find it.

428

My thoughts, feelings, beliefs, speeches, and words are not the truth.

You can perceive the truth only at the moment "YOU ARE" free from the slavery of your old thoughts, feelings, beliefs, speeches, and words.

429

Maybe you have asked yourself what the meaning of life is?

The answer to this question is straightforward --your existence is like a musical instrument.

First, it is essential to know what kind of musical instrument you are.

Second, you need to learn to play the instrument you are and use it as it is, not instead use it like other kinds of instruments that others are.

215

Third, the music of your presence will be manifested; only then you will be pure enthusiasm, ecstasy, and joy that is the meaning of your life.

In other words, your life will be meaningful; when everything you are in the depths of your heart and soul can shine and manifest in the physical world freely.

430

We do not have good and bad people.

Each one of us is a divine creature.

Maybe you ask about the criminal people.

They are divine creatures too; however, they are deeply sick emotionally.

You cannot treat sick people with punishment. It can only exacerbate their sickness.

They should be heavily treated with love and humanitarian values, and any discretion and liability shall be forfeited from them until the moment they get perfect health.

Those who cannot be cured must always be supervised by therapists, and their mental and physical ability to commit the crime must be paralyzed. Our first choices should not be to kill them or to paralyze the whole of their life and abilities in the prison system. They should be allowed to use their abilities to change their path and serve humanity.

However, there is a bigger problem. There are extremely sick people who can even become political, military, and religious leaders who obtain the authority to control millions of people. Worse is that most of the people know those leaders are sick, but still, they close their eyes to the truth and follow them to have little benefits like slaves.

The sick leaders may be responsible for thousands of crimes, but if they regret their mistake, most of the community blindly forgive them. However, the same community cannot forgive an ordinary criminal person whose crime is thousands of times less.

Opening your eyes for smaller crimes and closing them for more significant crimes according to who is more powerful, does not mean goodness; it is sickness too.

We do not have good and bad people. However, we are still divine creatures if we follow the truth deep inside our hearts and soul.

431

Living in the "here and now" is neither about accepting the reality even if it is inappropriate nor about accepting the limitations of time and space.

Living in the "here and now" means to be or trying to be at the moment YOU ARE original and where your HEART IS.

432

Most of you are in a hurry for a lifetime to become someone else who you are not and get things that are not yours, and you think this is being smart. Eventually, you will realize that you have destroyed someone who you were, and you lost the things that belonged to you.

All that you achieved was a mirage of success and happiness and a copy and fake identity and wealth which can never satisfy you deep inside your heart and soul.

Maybe sometimes, only for a fleeting time, you feel that your successes and wealth cannot make your life meaningful. This is not because your successes and wealth were worthless, but because they were not original for you, even if they were original for another one.

True happiness is not something we can fake. Unfortunately, this is what we learned to do in society.

True happiness must be original and comes from the shining of our originality.

433

When you truly and purely fall in love with someone, there is a moment in which your consciousness rises to a spiritual level, and you get a clear perception of the divinity of whom you love.

Her or his body is a temple, and their soul is what you amorously worship as a God or goddess.

Lovemaking between two people, who love each other honestly and purely, is a divine action beyond their bodies.

If you are not able to find divinity in the depth of another one's heart and soul, then there is no way to find it based on imaginations, illusions, and hallucinations.

434

Human beings are divine creatures, whether they realize it or not, and their aliveness is much more valuable than any belief.

If we have any belief that what we believe is more valuable than people's lives, then it is neither sacred nor divine.

435

You fall in love with someone once you reach the inner awareness that he or she is part of you and a divine creature whom you can achieve oneness together.

Inner enlightenment is the highest level of self-consciousness that you can understand the divineness and oneness of yourself and others, and you fall in love with anyone unconditionally.

A great and enlightened man or woman is not someone who is looking to show you that they are superior and more valuable than you, but someone who adores you like their beloved.

In simple words, the signs of the presence of a great and enlightened man or woman are that your feelings profoundly increase about divineness, adorableness, and loveliness of yourself.

436

You encounter much fake love in your life, and you conclude that love is worthless.

It would be best if you changed your viewpoint in the right direction. Already you know some people who purchase fake gold, diamonds, gems, and the most expensive things. These people know the criterion to measure their originality and purity. That's why fewer people can fake them.

Remember, there is no need to fake worthless things.

When you see many people fake love more than anything else, it exactly means that true love is more precious than anything else in this world.

When you do not try to know the criterion to measure originality and purity of the love you receive, or when you prefer to close your eyes to the fake love and try to paint it as true and pure love in your mind, then you face big problems.

The most potent acids cannot even destroy pure gold.

The most significant problems and considerable time and physical distances cannot even destroy pure love.

If the love fades under such circumstances, it is impure, but if it destroys, it is fake.

Remember, you cannot use the belief of "fake it till you make it" for the gold. It is the same about true love.

Maybe you can fake a good feeling and make it. However, true love is something quite different from the divine essence of your being, and you cannot fake it and make it.

It has a similar process for gold mining, but from the depths of your soul to manifest true love.

437

The foundations of political, economic, and belief systems are based on our separation and invisible slavery.

Our parents and past generations accepted this brainwashing as reality and convinced us that this is the truth.

All of those who have inner enlightenment clearly can make percept that this is a global scam somehow that even the scammers believe that it is the truth.

The truth is that we are all part of each other's oneness, divineness, and loveliness, and to achieve such an understanding is against the interests of political, economic and belief systems.

The systems that have most of the social power in the world and pretend to be the solution to human problems, but they are the biggest obstacle to manifest true and unconditional love to solve the problems of humanity.

We are like playful numbers for them. They try to make us believe and accept our separation and invisible slavery, then try to fake love, unity, greatness, and valuableness according to their interests to cover the truth.

438

Make-up and beautification have no contradiction with being original.

Everyone has the right to change his physical appearance by his or her inner world.

Being original does not mean unchanging your physical appearance. Being original must be based on the depth of your talents, interests, abilities, thoughts, and feelings, and if according to them, you enhance your body by applying make-up and you renovate your physical environment, they are incredibly good and acceptable.

But if your make-up and beautification is not in this direction and does not come from the depth of your existence and is not in harmony with the type of thought and feeling you have about yourself, but it is only to deceive yourself and others, in such a situation it is fake and inaccurate.

It should be noted that it does not matter whether beautification was completed with natural or unnatural materials. It only matters that make-up and beautification were based on inner states and your true thoughts and feelings toward yourself. Remember, it is critical to neither copy others nor to impersonate an appearance that is not in harmony with you within, because it merely diverts your attention and that of others from your true personality.

439

The death sentence and killing a human being is a crime. It originates from old and rotten beliefs.

It does not matter if it is executed by one person, a group or by government systems. In any case, this is a crime, and no matter what, their reason for killing a human being is wrong and outrageous.

222

We will all die one day and killing a human cannot be a punishment.

It is also not the solution to kill a criminal. Instead, it only cleanses the face of the problem without finding a real solution to prevent crime.

It is worth noting that crime is a result of severe mental and emotional illness. And many of these people are on the path of gradual suicide by themselves, wanted or unwanted, and they do not change the course of their lives when they see that another criminal has been executed.

Instead, for some criminals, this encourages them to commit more crimes.

Some religious people believe that they are particularly good people and are willing to kill another person in the name of God because they have concluded that some other humans are evil, and it is good and honorable if they kill the evil humans.

Likewise, a politician may kill different people, but for other reasons.

An ordinary criminal has his reasons for killing another, just as a religious or political or military person justifies his crime.

An ordinary criminal may also consider himself a good man who defends her/his and her/his family's rights, and s/he thinks if s/he kills a bad (or worse) person, s/he is doing the right thing.

There's a stark difference here. A religious person or a politician can commit some crimes and remain safe under the protection of robust religious, and political systems. However, an ordinary criminal has no support from a powerful system.

He or she is easily introduced to society as a bad man or woman by powerful systems.

These systems may define some beliefs and laws for a society that, because of human differences, society treats some people like criminals who are not criminals, but they can have a lot of positive practices.

I emphasize again that the death sentence and killing a human being is a crime. It does not matter if it is executed by one person, a group, or any governmental system. In any case, this is a crime and no matter what, their reason for killing a human being is, it is wrong and inhumane.

All this stems from the belief in good and bad and goodness and badness that is rooted in religious and political systems -- the belief that we are good, and others are bad made big problems for human society.

The truth of the world is not based on good or bad.

Everything is based on harmony or disharmony, and in nature, harmony does not mean "goodness," and disharmony does not mean "badness." They are not equal to being positive and negative, which is a measure of quantity for harmony and disharmony.

We are all divine beings.

If people commit crimes and inappropriate acts, it does not mean that they are bad, but rather it is a sign of self-alienation, identity disorder, and severe illness.

Under normal circumstances, such people should be limited and treated, and their subconscious mind scientifically must be reprogrammed to save other people's lives.

The main problem is when such sick people become religious and political leaders, and they spread their disease like a virus to the whole community to make them believe and accept it as reality.

This is what the human community suffers from in this world. In some societies, this is less and, in some other societies, more.

The first step in finding a solution and changing the situation is to become aware of the root of the significant problems of human society and to spread that awareness until the moment a widespread collective consciousness and civil disobedience to take power away from them, and the systems to be improved.

440

The underlying problems of human society are due to the ignorance of the difference between the two words of reality and the truth.

We have learned from childhood that our nation, race, language, gender, culture, thoughts, feelings, and beliefs are a fact that is the truth.

They may be based on temporal and spatial reality and the surrounding conditions, but they are definitely not the truth.

This is a huge mistake that has delimited human beings and has been the cause of many wars and bloodshed and crimes throughout history.

If you're a truth seeker, finally, you can get out of defined shells and experience your true self directly and without distortion.

Then you will realize that the truth is based on pure love and oneness, and we must respect each other's differences. The differences that each one of them is a piece of a global masterpiece puzzle. And by putting each puzzle piece in its place and completing the puzzle, we can manifest the universal truth together as one and by love.

There is no true love and no cure for the problems of human society until we realize the difference between reality and the truth and accept that the facts of our lives may not be the truth.

441

When we believe that killing is wrong, we cannot know it right for ourselves, because we think our goals are positive. The purpose does not justify the means because we can always make mistakes and our opinions throughout life can change many times and it can also happen to others.

No war is won based on the truth and justice but always based on the superior military, political, and economic powers in the same way that a deer can never win against a tiger.

Human society needs to go further than the old savagery principles to be able to step strongly and purely in the path of civilization and human values.

Killing people and executing them for political, religious, racial, and all other sorts of reasons in any form worldwide should be banned.

Humanity must reach such a level of consciousness that they stop using deadly weapons worldwide and replace them with anesthetic and temporary crippling weapons as defensive weapons against transgressors and invaders.

442

The extract of all of my messages to you is that you maybe have had weaknesses and mistakes in life, but now is the time to wake up!

Wake up deep down in your heart and soul, at the moment you can clearly understand who you truly are and that you are no one, but a free and lovely divine creature.

Whenever you realize this truth and are ready to manifest your freeness, loveliness, and divineness worldwide, you can find me to embrace each other's heart and soul and take the first step together to create a global love culture.

www.ingramcontent.com/pod-product-compliance
Lightning Source LLC
Chambersburg PA
CBHW031951080426
42735CB00007B/350